Man's Place in Nature

Man's Place in Nature

By Max Scheler

Translated, and with an Introduction, by

Hans Meyerhoff

THE NOONDAY PRESS
A Division of
FARRAR, STRAUS AND CUDAHY
New York

Contents

Translator's Preface   vii

Translator's Introduction   ix

Author's Preface   3

Introduction: The Concept of Man   5

I   The Stages of Psychophysical Life in Plant,
    Animal and Man   8

II   The Essence of Spirit   35

III   Spirit and Life   56

IV   Philosophical Anthropology and Religion   88

Notes   97

Index   101

translator's preface

In making this translation of *Man's Place in Nature*, I am deeply indebted to Dr. Julius S. Bixler, President Emeritus of Colby College. Dr. Bixler had prepared a translation of his own, and he kindly permitted me to use his version as the basis for my own work.

I have aimed at producing an English text that is as intelligible and readable as possible. There are still passages in this translation which do not satisfy me, but this basic aim explains some of the liberties I have taken with the original text. First, I have used both the edition of 1928 and the edition of 1947, which Maria Scheler published when her husband's works were again permitted to appear in Germany. The latter edition is, on the whole, an improvement over the first edition, but in several cases I have fallen back upon the edition of 1928 in order to choose a simpler wording or expression.

Again, for the sake of simplifying the text and the reading, I have made a few omissions. Since the German original appeared more than thirty years ago, the text contains a number of references to contemporary scientists and thinkers (usually just a name in parentheses) who then were an integral part of the scientific and intellectual scene in Germany, but who would now no longer be meaningful to the general reader even with the help of editorial footnotes. I have omitted a number of these parenthetical references and have retained only those that are still well-known or indispensable for an understanding of the text. I have also omitted a number of phrases, again usually parenthetical asides or repetitious rewordings in order to facilitate the flow and the progression of the sentential structure in English.

For the same reason, I have made a more drastic change. I have transferred some of the material which appears in the text to footnotes. I have done so reluctantly and in a few cases only, and I have indicated wherever I have made this change.

Finally, the division into four parts does not appear in the edition of 1947. In this edition, different sections of Scheler's essay are set off simply by wider spacing and asterisks.

These departures from the original text are based upon the sincere belief that they help in making Scheler's work more readable in English. I have often sacrificed felicity of expression when I thought the translation I would have preferred involved too radical a departure from the original.

I wish to thank Mrs. Ursula Sklarek for helping me in the final stages of revising this translation.

HANS MEYERHOFF

translator's introduction

I

Max Scheler died in 1928 at the age of fifty-four. He was a major thinker in contemporary philosophy; yet he has been a kind of forgotten man, and unjustly so.

In part, this neglect is due to the fact that Scheler's works were suppressed during the Nazi regime for racial reasons: his mother was Jewish, his father Catholic. A new edition of his complete works is now being published in Germany. Very little of his work has so far appeared in English, and very recently.[1] Meanwhile, other names in contemporary German philosophy have eclipsed Scheler's and many of his ideas have been appropriated by others and have passed into the intellectual climate of our times without due credit to their original source. It is fitting, therefore, to redress the historical balance in his favor. "Endowed with an unusual personality, Scheler was also beyond doubt the most brilliant thinker of his day."[2]

Whether or not this judgment will be confirmed by history, there is no doubt that, among his contemporaries,

[1] The Nature of Sympathy, *trans. Peter Heath, intro. W. Stark (London, 1954)*; and Philosophical Perspectives, *trans. Oscar A. Haac (Beacon Press: Boston, 1958)*.

[2] *I. M. Bocheński*, Contemporary European Philosophy (*University of California Press: Berkeley and Los Angeles, 1956*), *p. 140*.

Scheler was a unique thinker, for he combined the typically German genius for metaphysics with an impressive mastery of the empirical sciences. That is rare among German philosophers of our times. There is no one among them, except Ernst Cassirer, who shows Scheler's sense of responsibility toward empirical research in the human and social sciences, or who can compare with Scheler's technical competence and solid work in these disciplines. This odd blending of metaphysical ideas with scientific findings is perhaps the most striking characteristic of the essay *Man's Place in Nature*.

I shall say a few words about Scheler's personality—partly because it was very different from that of the ordinary academic philosopher, partly because it is a clue to the main currents of his thought.

The striking features of his character are those of a man of passion. He was charged with powerful emotions, driven by deep compulsions and torn by tragic inner conflicts. He was a restless soul—a Faustian man, as the Germans say—immersed in a ceaseless quest for new experiences and new knowledge. A superb intellect and tremendous learning seem to have been constantly at odds with the passions. In the language of Plato and his companions, Scheler was a deeply erotic thinker. He resembled Augustine and Pascal, and owed much to both in the development of his own thought.

Such a personality is relatively rare in the remote groves of academe. In 1910 Scheler resigned from the University of Munich and became a free-lance writer. During World War I, he was associated with the German Foreign Office; in the postwar period, he was a personal friend of Walter Rathenau's. Despite his great gifts and genuinely original contributions to philosophy, Scheler was in his forties when he won his first appointment, in 1919, to a regular academic chair at the University of Cologne. Throughout his life, he was an anomalous, controversial figure, an outsider in the professorial provinces, reminiscent of personalities like Peirce, Veblen or Russell.

He was also a very "interesting" person in the dual sense of being the focus of intense interests and of being immensely interested in all aspects of life. It has been said (in criticism) that Scheler projected his own self too much into his philosophy and, conversely, that he did not live up to his philosophical principles in his own life. There are few great thinkers in history of whom this could not be said, but it is true that Scheler often wrote in the heat of passion and prejudice, that he threw himself into controversial public issues (war, pacifism, the women's rights question, and so forth) that he often changed his mind—or seemed to because he was constantly trying to come to terms with incompatible attitudes within himself—and that he did not hesitate to use literary aphoristic or journalistic language in order to increase the persuasiveness of his arguments. He seems to have felt more deeply about the world he lived in, and exposed himself more vulnerably to its temptations and frustrations, than is generally the case with those who preach the doctrine of an existential commitment from the safe distance of their academic retreats.

This is not the place for a systematic and critical presentation of Scheler's thought,[3] but since *Man's Place in Na-*

---

[3] *In addition to Mr. Stark's introductory essay in* The Nature of Sympathy, *there is a careful analysis by Alfred Schutz of "Max Scheler's Epistemology and Ethics," I, II,* The Review of Metaphysics, *XI (1957–58), 304–314, 486–501.*

ture is his last work and represents the final phase of his philosophical world-view, we must say a few words about his intellectual background and development. As his personality was torn by the conflict between passion and intellect, so his thought was divided in its allegiance to antagonistic, incompatible influences.

There is both an impressive unity and a fatal split in the over-all structure of Scheler's work. Throughout his life, he pursued the same set of problems and responded with typical attitudes of mind. The constantly recurring question ("It occupied me from the first awakening of my philosophical consciousness") was: "What is man?" In the essay, "Man and History," Scheler expressed himself more dramatically: "In the ten thousand years of history, we are the first age in which man has become utterly and unconditionally 'problematic' to himself, in which he no longer knows who he is, but at the same time *knows that* he does not know. It is only by a firm resolution to wipe the canvas clean of all traditional answers . . . and to look upon man with a radical, methodological alienation and astonishment that we can again hope to gain some valid insights." If these words have a familiar ring, it is because they have been so frequently copied and adapted.

Scheler hoped to gain some new insights about man in three areas: (1) in relation to a realm of values, both ethical and religious; (2) in relation to society, history and culture; (3) in relation to man's place in the universe of living things. These three fields encompass the domain of his philosophy.

This unified pattern of inquiry, however, was constantly threatened by deeply divided intellectual loyalties.

For, in addition to Augustine and Pascal, and the tradition of German idealism—which is a *sine qua non* for any philosophical training in Germany—the major intellectual influences upon Scheler were twofold and antagonistic.

One was the movement known as the "philosophies of life," for which Nietzsche, Bergson and Dilthey were the most famous spokesmen. The other was the philosophical movement known as "phenomenology." The meeting with Edmund Husserl, in the first years of this century, was a decisive event in Scheler's intellectual development. Next to Husserl himself, Scheler became the most powerful mind in launching the phenomenological movement and its increasingly influential philosophical journal. The two men divided, by inclination and temperament, the world for phenomenological analysis: Husserl's chief contributions being in epistemology, logic, mathematics and the sciences in general; Scheler's chief contributions being in ethics, religion, psychology and sociology—in other words, the human world in general.

Scheler did not, I think, ever succeed in fusing these divergent influences. The philosophies of life pulled him in the direction of naturalism, vitalism and historicism, and aligned him with the empirical disciplines concerned with man and society. The concept of "life," however vague and ambiguous it might be, became a unifying agent in his thinking as it did, say, in Nietzsche's philosophy. Thus all the manifestations of life—from life in nature to life in man, from the irrational, unconscious roots of vital drives to the most sublime sublimations in human culture, from technology to ideology, from biology to sociology, from science to religion—were different aspects of the same processes in nature which could be studied and comprehended in their evolution, differentiation and dynamic interaction.

The other influence, phenomenology, pulled Scheler in the opposite direction, for it repudiated this kind of naturalism as well as any other kind of "ism" in philosophy. Phenomenology is now a major philosophical movement in our times. It represents quite a radical shift in contemporary thought, and it has had momentous consequences in philosophy and in a number of other disciplines. Heidegger, a disciple and successor of Husserl's, scored his spectacular success, in *Sein und Zeit,* by employing and partly modifying a phenomenological method; a similar approach is used in many other areas of contemporary philosophy not directly associated with Husserl's type of phenomenology.[4] Phenomenology involves highly technical issues that cannot be discussed here; I mention only two characteristic features of this new look in philosophy because they enter into the present work.

The first is expressed in Husserl's maxim: "Back to the things themselves." He meant the "things" as they appear, that is, the "phenomena." In this sense, phenomenology is a radical and naïve empiricism. It sets out to study the human world as it appears to the ordinary observer or as we encounter it in direct, immediate experience. This human

---

4 *Even the recent revival—or revolution—in English philosophy, Oxford Linguistic Philosophy, falls into this category; for, as one of its leading spokesmen explained, it is best understood as a kind of "linguistic phenomenology." (Phenomenology has found its way into a number of nonphilosophical disciplines as well, e.g., anthropology, psychology, sociology, and religion.) I have dealt with some of these methodological affinities in contemporary thought in an essay, "The Return of the Concrete"* (Chicago Review, Summer *1959*).

world, again, is the ordinary world in which we live, work and play every day.[5] Thus the slogan says: The things, or phenomena, which we find and encounter in this world must be taken at their face value; they must be judged in their own terms, as we experience them, without being prejudged in terms of some scientific theory of abstract concepts of philosophy. In another sense, phenomenology refers to the method employed in this study. This method is purely, or predominantly, descriptive. Thus the rule also says: Let us first describe and record what we find in the world of human experience before we think and theorize about it. Let us describe the qualities, objects and relations in the world as they appear to an unprejudiced observer or to a mind uncontaminated by science or philosophy, before we try to explain and interpret what we find according to some general theory. Theories may explain and interpret the world, but they also *abstract* from the objects and meanings as we encounter them in the field of immediate experience. They also alienate the human mind from its natural habitat in the world. We murder to dissect. Or, less dramatically, we may be blind to the "things" in experience because we see them only through the abstract glasses of some scientific or philosophical theory. Scheler's analysis of instinct, behaviorism, and the nature of spiritual acts are instances of employing a phenomenological method in the present work.

The second stage of a phenomenological analysis is the method of "reduction." This is not, I believe, as great a discovery as its proponents have often claimed it is, for behind the new word stands an old philosophical practice. It is the

[5] *Husserl's term for this world is* Lebenswelt; *Heidegger's is* Dasein.

practice of going from the manifold qualities and objects in experience to an intellectual intuition of their "essences" (*Wesensschau*). These essences are a priori, that is, they are believed to yield objective and universally valid insights into the hidden structures and meanings behind the phenomenal world. As Scheler explains in the present essay, "the capacity to separate 'essence' from 'existence' is the fundamental characteristic of the human spirit." He suggests that mathematics provides the richest field for the intuition of such essences, but he also tries to show how Buddha hit upon the essence of pain, or how Descartes elicited the essence of matter in his famous experiment with a piece of wax. Thus, this kind of reduction, or the intellectual intuition of essences, is believed to be the philosophical method par excellence, for the essences reveal truths different from scientific knowledge. They are a priori, not empirical; they are universally valid, not probable; they are insights into "essential" meanings, not propositions based upon causal analysis and explanation as in the sciences.

These two intellectual sources are felt throughout Scheler's work, and the split, first concealed and repressed, finally breaks out into open conflict. The phenomenological method prevails in his work on psychology, ethics and religion until about 1921. The naturalistic tendencies of his thought reassert themselves increasingly in his works on sociology, history and philosophical anthropology from 1921 until his death.

In his first major work, *Der Formalismus in der Ethik und die materiale Werthethik* (*Formalism in Ethics and an Ethics of Objective Values*, 1916) Scheler proclaimed the simple, yet radical, thesis that "values" be given the same objective and autonomous status in nature as sensory qualities or material objects. Even as sense-perception confronts us directly with a thing-world in our experience, so our feelings make accessible to us a realm of value objects, both ethical and aesthetic. Against psychological theories of values, Scheler argued that a phenomenological analysis of these values reveals that they are altogether different, in their specific nature, from the subjective states of feeling, which may or may not accompany them. Against Kant's "formalism in ethics," he argued that this realm of objective values is the foundation, or presupposition, for any moral imperative or for any formal principles of obligation.

These ideas have much in common with the views of other recent thinkers like F. Brentano G. E. Moore or W. Köhler, who defended the objective status of values. What distinguished Scheler was that he moved beyond this initial analysis to assert that, within this realm of values, there was an essential, a priori order of preference which could be laid bare by a phenomenological reduction. In short, there is a *logique du coeur* as there is a logic of the intellect; there is an "emotional apriorism" as there are a priori categories of the understanding. The order of preference runs as follows: (1) values of sensible feeling (pleasant and unpleasant); (2) values of vital feeling (noble and vulgar); (3) spiritual values (beautiful and ugly, just and unjust); (4) religious values (holy and unholy).[6]

Feelings, being the feelers which link us with the value-charged presence of reality, are also the means for gaining access to the allegedly private worlds of other minds, as Scheler tried to show in *The Nature of Sympathy*. This

[6] *Cf. I. M. Bocheński, op. cit., pp. 145–46.*

study runs parallel to the ethical treatise. Feelings make values accessible to us; love makes them known to us. Thus Scheler here presents a ladder of love, in the tradition of the *Symposium,* corresponding to the hierarchical order of values: from physical love on the level of vital values, to love of God on the level of the value of the holy. The work is an orthodox phenomenological analysis of love, hate, sympathy, pity, and so on, and a running criticism of metaphysical and naturalistic theories of the emotions (including Freud's). It is full of ideas that again have a familiar ring because they have been picked up and elaborated elsewhere, as in the writings of Jaspers, Sartre, Merleau-Ponty and L. Binswanger. But in addition to these merits, there are two points which, I think, deserve special mention.

One is Scheler's restatement of the Platonic-Augustinian view that love is an instrument of knowledge. The other has a more technical application to philosophy because it concerns the problem of "other minds."

How do we know them, or, how do we know that, behind the overt behavior, language and gestures of others, there are minds or souls like our own? By inference, by analogy, by empathy or by some other means that will get us out of the private prison of our own selves? Scheler rejects all these "inferential" arguments—or turns them around. The problem as stated in these arguments is a pseudo-problem. It is generated by a false, prejudicial reading of reality. For it proceeds on the assumption that we first know only our own selves and must grope our way to the knowledge of others with the help of some artificial theory. Instead, the knowledge of other minds is given prior to the knowledge of our own. We have direct access to other minds because, to begin with—say, as children—they form as integral a part of our immediate experience as anything else in the world. It would be more correct to say that we discover our own selves by "inference," in other words, by detaching and differentiating them from the community of other minds in which we are originally immersed. These ideas, by now quite familiar from other studies, were not unworthy insights when first put forth in 1913.

Phenomenological realism is also the basis for Scheler's major work in religious philosophy, *Vom Ewigen im Menschen* (*On the Eternal in Man*).[7] As there is a general realm of values corresponding to the objects sought out, or "intended by" our feelings, so there is a special realm of the holy corresponding to our religious feelings and acts. Again, the phenomenological analysis consists in taking the contents of this religious world at their face value. Again, the phenomenological reduction consists in laying bare the essential, a priori structure of the religious world; for example, the essential difference between philosophy and religion, the specific characteristics of the divine essence (*ens a se, summum bonum,* holiness, infinity, omnipotence), or the specific significance of religious acts. The religious outlook is strictly theistic and Catholic, though Augustinian rather than Thomist. The work has been widely discussed in Catholic literature, but it contains a thought which is often cited in other contexts as well. According to Scheler, man has no choice about being religious or not. The only choice he has is with regard to the object intended by his religious acts. Worship he must; but he may worship either *Gott* or *Götze* —God or an idol.

[7] [1921.] On the Eternal in Man (*SCM Press: London, 1960*).

The religious treatise marks a turning point in Scheler's life and thought, for having completed it, he disowned it. The loss of faith was a sign of a fundamental shift all along the intellectual front. It was a turning-point in the literal sense, a return of intellectual sources which had been held back by his "faith" in phenomenology as if, even in the world of ideas, there were such a thing as a return of the repressed.

After 1921, the conflict between the naturalistic and phenomenological components in Scheler's thought broke out into the open. The struggle contributed to his best works in sociology, history and philosophical anthropology. All of them are torn between a philosophy of life and phenomenology. All of them reflect a deep conflict of loyalties: an increasing recognition of the material and social conditions determining human existence, and the relevance of empirical studies in the human sciences, on the one hand, and Scheler's allegiance to a phenomenological analysis in philosophy, on the other. Perhaps Scheler rediscovered the roots of his own passionate nature—and, by this channel, the material roots of man in nature and society. At any rate, he came to acknowledge that philosophy cannot, and must not, neglect man's place "in nature" if it is to make a contribution to human knowledge beyond the discovery of "essences" in the ethereal realm of pure speculation.

In relation to culture and history, these newly discovered "material factors" (*Realfaktoren*) were twofold: (1) material conditions, such as geography, climate, race, population pressure, economic resources and technology; (2) the basic biological drives for self-preservation, power and sex. In other words, Scheler tried to incorporate Darwin and Marx as well as Nietzsche and Freud into the structure of his thought. He now conceded that all naturalistic theories of culture and history were right in assigning a crucial and autonomous role to these *Realfaktoren*. They are necessary conditions, (a) because they are subject to a causality of their own, and (b) because they determine the fate of ideas in history.

Yet, Scheler tried to remain faithful to his idealistic and phenomenological past as well. The spirit of man and its products—which he called the "ideal factors" (*Idealfaktoren*)—were not completely reducible to these material conditions. They were not simply an ideological superstructure: "It would be a mistake to say that the material factors in history unequivocally determine the contents and meaning of a spiritual culture. They merely determine the realization (*Auswirkung*) of spiritual potentialities." In short, the material factors serve as principles of selection. They limit the range of ideal possibilities that can be realized in any given historical situation. Thus Scheler's last great works are another—and, I think, impressive—attempt to mediate between materialistic and idealistic conceptions of history.

This mediation was not easy, and often broke down; for while Scheler clung to the idealistic thesis that ideas have an objective, independent status of their own, he also adopted the view that these products of the spirit were so "pure" that they were helpless vis-à-vis the forces of nature. The spirit has no "positive creative power" of its own; it can acquire such power only by "sublimation." It must convert emotional impulses into spiritual energy. Ideas may have their own validity, meaning and value, but they can become weapons in history only if they align themselves with material conditions and instinctual forces. For its active participation in the world, the spirit only has as much *power* as it has withdrawn from the vital, emotional sources of energy. "Wherever ideas do not find objective forces, interests, passions and drives, they are completely ineffectual in history." Marx was right in his critique of Hegel: ideas without the support of material conditions make fools of themselves in reality.

Yet, in this alliance through which ideas become effective in the world of action, they are also debased and degraded. The spirit always loses in its contest with nature. The "higher" forms of being, the "nobler" truths, are also the weaker. They invariably succumb to the superior power of the lower forces in nature and of the vulgar truths in history.

Since the concrete expressions of man's spirit are invariably determined by the *Realfaktoren* in history, there emerges a special field of inquiry which studies the dependence of ideas upon the existential and social roots of man's being. This study Scheler called the "sociology of knowledge" and devoted two major works to it: *Schriften zur Soziologie und Weltanschauungslehre* (*Essays in Sociology and Philosophical World Views,* 1923–1924) and *Die Wissensformen und die Gesellschaft* (*Forms of Knowledge and Society,* 1926). He did not, of course, discover the idea of a sociology of knowledge. What he did was to perceive that this idea could, and should, be developed, outside the context of Marx and Nietzsche, in the form of a specialized sociological and historical discipline. Again, he has received far too little recognition for this step; it was Karl Mannheim who got most of the credit.

Two aspects of Scheler's work along these lines are worth mentioning in particular. First, the concept of "knowledge" may be analyzed within an existential, historical context. Such an analysis yields different meanings, or *types*, of knowledge according to the function they serve. One type is that which we now associate with scientific knowledge. It is a knowledge of domination and achievement, a *Herrschafts-* and *Leistungswissen,* and it serves the purpose of extending and increasing man's power over nature and in society. This type of knowledge, based as it is on the experimental sciences, has now prevailed in Western culture. The second type of knowledge is more ancient. It corresponds to what Aristotle called "First Philosophy," or metaphysics. It consists of a knowledge of "essences" which provide the metaphysical foundations of the positive sciences and which are a clue to the spiritual nature of man. Scheler called this *Bildungswissen.* The third type of knowledge is religious knowledge, or the knowledge of "Absolute Being" (God) for the sake of salvation or redemption, *Heils-* and *Erlösungswissen.*

Secondly, the idea of man may be analyzed in an existential, historical context. Such an analysis again yields different types, or images, of man. In the essay, "Man and History," Scheler distinguished five dominant types in history: *Homo religiosus, Homo sapiens, Homo faber,* man as the failure of "life," and man as the *Übermensch.* This typology of human nature was both a prelude to, and an offshoot from, an inquiry to which Scheler, at the end of his life, assigned "the greatest urgency": a study of the nature of man in relation to his "biological, psychological, ideological and social development." This is what he meant by a "philosophical anthropology." It was predicated upon the Hegelian thesis that history is the record of man's progressive self-consciousness. A philosophical anthropology, therefore, would answer the central question—"What is man?"—by raising to the level of self-consciousness man's knowledge of himself as it has developed in "language, technology, the state, the arts, myth, religion, science, history, and communal life."

This is the big work that Scheler did not live to write. Instead, he wrote the vast fragment of *Man's Place in Nature* (1928) and a series of essays collected under the title of *Philosophical Perspectives* (1929).[8] These last works depict the inner split in Scheler's thought and nature in its purest form. They are torn by the conflict between "life" and "spirit" (*Geist*), between man as a child of nature and society, on the one hand, and his capacity for (phenomenological) philosophy, on the other. There is, of course, nothing new about the conflict itself. It is as old as Plato's dualism or as new as the romantic (and existentialist) search for reconciling nature and spirit. It is too easy a criticism to say that Scheler failed to solve the problem that haunted him throughout his life: the problem of modern man who does not know who he is, but knows that he does not know. His own failure is but a dramatic reminder of other efforts that have failed to solve the same dilemma. Thus, like Lord Jim, Scheler is one of us in that he reminds us of our common intellectual heritage and *échec*.

[8] *This volume cited above contains two essays, "Philosopher's Outlook," and "Man and History," in which Scheler expounds his theory of the different types of knowledge and the different images of man in history. Cf. footnote 1.*

In an over-all estimate of Scheler's philosophical achievements, there are those who think that he reached his greatest heights in his studies before 1921, and that his work declined to the degree to which he departed, in his later years, from the straight and narrow path of phenomenology. There are others, and I belong to them myself, who may find his later studies in historical sociology and philosophical anthropology more exciting and rewarding precisely because Scheler rediscovered in them the legitimate claims of life against the isolation and alienation of the spirit.

II

Written under the judgment of death, *Man's Place in Nature* is a rough, fragmentary draft for a work which was never written. This explains its virtues as well as its defects. It is packed with ideas that would ordinarily fill a book or more. It shows Scheler's remarkable grasp and mastery of the literature in various scientific disciplines. It reveals his skill in condensing this material and in concentrating upon the philosophical issues at stake. At the same time, the essay is written in a style and language which are forbidding and which pose unusually great difficulties for the translator. Chapters are compressed into pages; paragraphs, into sentences; and the sentences often lose themselves in an architectonic maze which is impenetrable even in the original. It is as if Scheler knew that this was his last chance.

Since *Man's Place in Nature* presents special problems and makes special demands, I propose, at the risk of being pedantic, to unpack some of its major themes and to put them, with appropriate comments, into a simplified schema. Thus these comments are in the nature of an outline with personal footnotes and I should hope that they may be helpful both before and after reading the text of the essay.

A brief prelude deals with the "deceptive ambiguity" in the concept of man. We use the word "man," on the one hand, to refer to a being that is part of the world of living things in general. In scientific discourse, the human species is simply another branch of the animal kingdom. On the other hand, we seem to use words like "man" or "human" in order to designate something that is radically different from anything we find in the animal world and among living things in general.

This ambiguity sets the stage for two questions: What does man have in common with other living things, and what, if anything, makes him unique? These questions are discussed in parts I (pages 8–34) and II (pages 35–55) of the essay. There follows a third part (pages 56–87), in which the results of the previous analysis are worked out in a critical exchange with other theories. And there is a brief coda, in which the results are applied to the problem of religion or God (pages 88–95).

Part I is a detailed and compact survey of the "structure of the biopsychological world." It proceeds on several assumptions: (1) As in Aristotle, the terms "psychic" and "living" are used interchangeably; thus wherever there is "life," there is a "psychic" principle. (2) The word "psychic" includes not only characteristics like self-movement or self-differentiation, but also, as for Hegel or Sartre, a special quality of "being-for-itself." (3) Man contains in himself all the essential psychic structures developed in the process of evolution. The first part, then, is a sketch of these "essential" forms of life—of which there are four—culminating in man. It is this part in which Scheler expresses his allegiance to the naturalism of modern science and the philosophies of life.

The first and lowest stage in the evolutionary development of the psyche is an undifferentiated vital impulse or drive (*Gefühlsdrang*); a kind of *conatus,* in Spinoza's language; a blind will, as in Schopenhauer; an *élan vital,* as in Bergson; or a non-specific kind of libido in more recent terminology. It is (1) unconscious, (2) without impressions and (3) without a central feedback mechanism. It is the characteristic mode of plant life. In describing its behavior, Scheler uses the odd term "ec-static." He means that the plants are completely "outward-bound," as it were, and fixated in their natural environment. They have not yet developed a psychic structure which turns "inward" and "backwards" upon itself (*reflexio*) and subordinates the partial response systems to a minimum of inner control over the *whole* organism.

This primitive life-force plays a crucial role in two respects: First, it is the only source of psychic energy throughout the evolutionary process. It reaches up into the highest forms of human life. Even the human spirit must draw upon it in order to become "alive." "There is no feeling, no perception, no idea into which this dark impulse does not enter." Secondly, it is also the source for the most primitive sense of "reality." Following Dilthey, Scheler attributes this sense of reality to the "resistance" which the environment puts up against the inner drives. As John Dewey once put it more simply: "Objects," to begin with, are things that "object."

The second stage is what Scheler calls instinctual behavior. Behavior is instinctual if it is (1) purposive for the organism as a whole, (2) rhythmic, (3) responsive to recurring situations indispensable for the survival of the species, (4) innate and (5) inheritable. Instinctual behavior is the first mode of differentiation and specialization in the psychic structure.

All higher forms of life are the result of such a process of "dissociation"—which corresponds, on the physiological level, to a shift from subcortical to cortical processes. This has two important consequences: First, the function of the human mind, according to Scheler, is not primarily "synthetic," as Kant and others believed. The mind is not needed to put together isolated and unrelated bits of experience to construct a meaningful world. Instead, its function is "analytic," that is, to break up and differentiate components which, on the level of non-reflective, immediate experience, are invariably given as parts of "whole" and meaningful structures. Secondly, even instinctual behavior exhibits this "wholeness" or *Gestalt* quality and cannot be completely resolved into mechanistic or associative models.

Two further manifestations of psychic life emerge from a differentiation of instinctual behavior. The third form is "associative" behavior or memory. It corresponds to the conditioned reflex, or to the separation of the sensory from the motor system through the development of the reflex arc. It signifies a liberation from the instinctual type of response in that, though relatively fixed, it is the result of a learning process and modifiable on the basis of quantitative reinforcements. It is characteristic of life in animals, but is most highly developed in man and it plays a crucial role in social life. Scheler cites Hume's mechanisms of association by "contiguity" and "resemblance," but adds that there are no *pure* associations: They are always conditioned by drives and needs, even by intellectual factors.

Practical intelligence is the fourth major type of psychic life. It consists of a problem-solving response, that is, a new, unlearned response, an "Aha-experience," which occurs suddenly and independently of the number of trial runs. Animals have this intelligence, as well as the rudiments of deliberate choice, because they are complex, self-regulating, feedback systems capable of exercising a considerable degree of central control over their partial reflex and response patterns. Yet, although animals have achieved this complex, inner organization, their primary mode of existence, in contrast to man, is still "ec-static," relatively fixed and immersed in the environment.

Thus ends the first part of the essay. It should be evident that, in the discussion and interpretation of the scientific material, Scheler owes most to Nietzsche, Bergson and biological or psychological studies that emphasize a *Gestalt* and teleological point of view. In his method, he tries to employ a neutral, phenomenological description.

The second part of the essay owes an obvious debt to German idealism and to phenomenology. It opens with a crucial question: In the light of this common heritage and evolutionary development of "life" throughout nature, is there anything but a difference in *degree* between man and the animal world? Is there still a difference in *kind* or "essence"?

Faithful to the idealistic tradition, Scheler discovers such a difference in the principle of the spirit (*Geist*). The spirit of man is radically different from, and opposed to, all manifestations of life, including the natural dispositions toward intelligent behavior and deliberate choice. Its "essence" is a sense of freedom transcending all conditions in nature.

Freedom means the capacity of detaching oneself from the natural conditions of life in two respects: (1) from the conditions in the psychophysical organism itself, and (2) from the natural life in, and automatic response to, the environment. The former act defines the nature of self-consciousness; the latter creates an "objective" attitude toward the world. Both acts are correlative.

Self-consciousness is described as an act of "concentration" (*Sammlung*), a meta-reflex action, as it were, upon the central psychic switchboard. As for Kant, self-consciousness and the capacity for "objectifying" one's world are complementary functions of "the same, indissoluble psychic structure in man." Thus, it is the same act of concentration by which the psychic structure of man becomes conscious of its own processes and by which the natural world view is transformed into a field consisting of "objects" in the technical, scientific sense. The processes of the mind become "objects" for scientific study as in psychology. The phenomena in the natural world become material things in space and time. Man not only lives in a world, he also *has* a world; or, to be more precise, he has the capacity for an unlimited "openness" to, and detachment from, the natural world. It is this capacity which enables him to restructure this world in terms of abstract categories like substance and number, space and vacuum, time and causality, which are the theoretical foundations and basic tools for science and philosophy.

These ideas are more or less in the idealistic tradition. To phenomenology Scheler owes the view that "spiritual acts"—analogous to acts of perception—are "intentional." As acts of perception "intend," or directly disclose to us a world of objective phenomena (or objective values), so the spiritual acts *aim at* revealing the essential structure of this phenomenal world. Husserl's concept of "intellectual intuition" (*Wesensschau*) reappears as the process of "ideation" —hardly distinguishable from abstraction. The capacity "to isolate essence from existence" is now said to be "the fundamental characteristic of the human spirit" from which all others are derived. The spirit is, to rephrase Kant, a kind of transcendental unity of intentional acts. Its center is called the "person."

Scheler's own contribution to this analysis is to link the process of ideation with the process of sublimation. The phenomenological reduction according to his view, and different from Husserl's, is an act of canceling the primitive sense of "reality" which accompanies the experience of "resistance" felt in the encounter between the libidinal drives and the natural environment. To cancel this sense of reality, therefore, means to cancel and negate the efficacy of the vital impulses. Thus the spirit, in essence, is also a *Geist, der stets verneint,* a negative, Mephistophelian principle, and instrument of repression; in short, the great "nay-sayer" to life. A spiritual act is an "ascetic" act. It inhibits, deflects or lures the libido from its natural goals in order to acquire some vital energy for its own "ideas." Without the repressed energy withdrawn from "life" in this process of sublimation the spirit is impotent and inoperative.

Thus life and spirit are poised in radical opposition and dependence. The spirit enjoys an autonomous, ontological status in the structure of Being. In "essence," it is completely different from life. In "reality," however, it is completely dependent on it, for the spirit becomes "alive" only through the energy which it has withdrawn from the passions.

Part III is an elaboration of the crucial theme of this dualism. It deals with two main topics: (1) spirit and sublimation, and (2) the psychophysical monism of body and soul and the metaphysical dualism of life and spirit.

In the first section (pages 56–71) Scheler compares his own views on life and spirit with two other theories: (1) the "classical" theory, according to which the spirit, mind, reason or *nous* are the highest forms of being and power in the universe—God being the supreme "spirit"—and (2) the "negative" theory, according to which the spirit of man is *nothing but* sublimated life-force or libido.

The classical theory appears in two forms: as the doctrine of a substantial soul in man, and as the doctrine of a universal world-soul. The crucial error in both versions is the assertion, or unproved assumption, that the "higher" forms of psychic life are not only more valuable, but also more powerful. Against this classical view, Scheler sides with the naturalistic theories in the modern world. The most powerful agencies in man are his drives and vital impulses. "All higher categories of being and value are by nature the weaker ones." They are invariably distorted and contaminated by the superior power of the lower categories of being in man and nature. Applied to the social world, this view leads to the dialectics between "ideal" and "material" factors in history, which I have briefly sketched.[9]

Buddha, Schopenhauer and Freud are the major representatives of what Scheler calls the negative theory of the spirit. Against them he raises the crucial question: What is it that negates the will to life? What is it that represses the drives? In short, his criticism is that these theories invariably presuppose, or take for granted, something like "spirit," which they set out to explain in terms of biological impulses or instincts. Scheler's interpretation of these theories may not always be correct, but his central question, I think, does point to a legitimate difficulty. Naturalistic theories seem to assume that there is some autonomous center of energy, whether it be called ego, self, person or what not, which functions independently and self-regulatively in the psychobiological structure of man in order to counteract and rechannel libidinal energies, or in order to initiate and sustain processes of repression and sublimation.

Scheler confined the activity of the spirit to the "direction" (inhibition) and "guidance" (displacement) of libidinal energy. He did not explain how and why these mechanisms work. He did not work out a detailed model which would explain the manifold transformations and dynamic interactions between life and spirit. Sometimes he seems to suggest that the spirit lures the instincts from their natural goals by a special "cunning" of its own; at other times (for example, on page 54), he writes as if the spirit did have some power of its own, after all; for how could it initiate the act of repression if it were nothing but "pure intentionality"?

[9] See p. xxxii of this volume.

The second section [10] serves several purposes: It clarifies the nature of Scheler's dualism. Instead of the traditional dualism of body and soul, we now have the "metaphysical dualism" of life and spirit. As to the relationship between body and soul, Scheler adopts a strict organismic monism or psychophysical parallelism. Life is a psychophysical unity. "Physiological and psychic processes are ontologically *identical*," which means that they are only different modes of the same unitary process of life, that they are easily interchangeable, as evidenced by psychosomatic ailments, and that they differ only in their appearances or phenomenological characteristics.

Next, this section serves to distinguish Scheler's views both from "naturalistic" and from "pan-romantic" theories of life and spirit. Since there are romantic and anti-intellectual tendencies in Scheler's own thought, he is anxious to dissociate himself from an extreme position along these lines, especially from the ideas of Ludwig Klages and others cited in the text. It is to his credit to have sensed the dangers inherent in this resurgence of irrationalism in modern culture. He opposed what he called "overintellectualization" and "oversublimation," but he reaffirmed, in the spirit of Nietzsche and Freud, the primacy of the spirit even though its voice be feeble and weak. He repudiated the trend— which has greatly increased since his time—of glorifying the irrational, unconscious powers of life and of hailing them as the harbingers of wisdom and salvation beyond the feeble powers of man's spirit and intellect.

Finally, this section continues a discussion which goes to the heart of the matter: whether it is possible to reconcile the dualism of life and spirit. Scheler's answer may be found

[10] *See pp. 71–87.*

wanting. In fact, the task he set himself may be hopeless, for how can man join together what in "essence" is rendered asunder? But if his own solution leaves much to be desired, he also knew that other theories were beset by difficulties.

The brief coda on which the essay ends is biographically interesting because it represents Scheler's break with orthodox theism, whether Catholic or otherwise. In content, I believe, it is the least original part of the essay. Spinoza's pantheism and Bergson's creative evolution fuse in Scheler's concept of the "self-deification" of man. With the death of God in the religious sense, man becomes God. Hegel's idea of the self-realization of Reason in history now reappears, in the context of a creative pantheism, as the self-realization of God in man and history. God is constantly "becoming" in man to the extent to which mankind realizes its own spiritual potentialities or transforms natural resources and vital energies into products of the spirit.

In the end, Scheler practically admits that his own solution to the metaphysical dilemma posed by *Man's Place in Nature* is an act of faith. He pleads for his basic conviction that life and spirit are not antagonistic, but complementary principles in nature, and that there is an inherent movement in man, in history and in the Absolute Being itself whereby the passions are "spiritualized" and the spirit becomes "alive." But these pleadings are neither arguments nor "theoretical certainties." The dilemma is not resolved in a theoretical context, but by an existential leap. An act of commitment solves the problem of "knowing." This may be an odd way out of the dilemma which Scheler has conjured up in this essay, but if we are honest, we might also admit that we have come no closer to a solution than he did.

man's place in nature

author's preface

The questions "What is man?" and "What is man's place in the nature of things?" have occupied me more deeply than any other philosophical question since the first awakening of my philosophical consciousness. Efforts of many years during which I have attacked this problem from all possible sides have come together, since 1922, in the composition of a major work devoted to this inquiry. I have had the good fortune to see that most of the philosophical work I had done previously has culminated in this study.*

Many people have expressed the wish that the lecture entitled "The Unique Place of Man," which I delivered in April 1927 at the School of Wisdom in Darmstadt, appear in published form. I hereby comply with this wish.

This essay represents a brief and highly condensed summary of my views on some of the main topics of the "Philosophical Anthropology" on which I have been at work for a number of years and which will appear early in 1929. In my lectures at the University of Cologne between 1922 and 1928, I have presented the results of my research frequently and in much more detail than in this cursory survey.

I am pleased to see that the problems of philosophical anthropology are in the center of philosophical reflections in

* [*Scheler did not live to complete or publish this major work.* **Trans.**]

Germany today and that, outside philosophical circles, biologists, medical men, psychologists and sociologists are at work on a new model for the essential structure of man.

In spite of this, however, man is more of a problem to himself at the present time than ever before in all recorded history. At the very moment when man admits that he knows less than ever about himself, and when he is not frightened by any possible answer to the question, there seems to have arisen a new courage of truthfulness—a courage to raise this essential question without any commitment to any tradition, whether theological, philosophical or scientific, that has prevailed up to now. At the same time, he is developing a new kind of self-consciousness and insight into his own nature based on the vast accumulation of knowledge in the new human sciences.

Max Scheler

introduction: the concept of man

If we ask an educated person in the Western world what he means by the word "man," three irreconcilable ways of thinking are apt to come into conflict in his mind. The first is the Jewish-Christian tradition of Adam and Eve, including creation, paradise and fall. The second is the Greek tradition in which, for the first time, man's self-consciousness raised him to a unique place on the grounds that he is endowed with "reason." * Closely bound up with this view is the doctrine that there is a superhuman "reason" in the total universe in which man alone of all creatures participates. The third idea is that of modern science and genetic psychology, which also has a tradition of its own. According to this view, man is a very recent product of evolution on our planet, a creature distinguished from its antecedents in the animal world only by the degree of complexity of energies and capacities already present on a subhuman level. These three ideas are not compatible with each other. Thus we have a scientific, a philosophical and a theological anthropol-

* Vernunft, logos, phronesis, ratio, mens.—Logos *here means both speech and the capacity to grasp the nature of things.* [*In the original this passage occurs in the text. Trans.*]

ogy in complete separation from each other. We do not have a unified idea of man.

The increasing multiplicity of the special sciences that deal with man, valuable as they are, tend to hide his nature more than they reveal it. Moreover, since the status of these three traditional ideas is severely impaired, in particular the Darwinian theory of the origin of man, we may say that at no time in his history has man been so much of a problem to himself as he is now. For this reason I have tried to give an outline of a new philosophical anthropology based on as broad a foundation as possible. In the following essay, however, I want to raise only a few issues and suggest a few conclusions that deal with the nature of man in relation to animal and plant and with man's unique metaphysical place in the universe.

In setting out upon this inquiry, we must be aware that the word "man" has a deceptive ambiguity. In one sense, it signifies the particular morphological characteristics of man as a subclass of the vertebrates and mammals. It is perfectly clear that, regardless of the specific form of this conceptual model, the living being described as man is not only subordinate to the concept "animal," but occupies a relatively very small corner of the animal kingdom. This is the case even if we say with Linnaeus that man is the "pinnacle" of the vertebrate-mammal kingdom—an assertion, in itself highly debatable, since this pinnacle, like any other, still belongs to the line of development of which it is the highest point. This view derives a unified concept of man from the upright posture, the transformation of the vertebral column, equilibration of the brain pan, the big increase in the relative size of the brain and the organic changes resulting from the upright posture: the grasping hand with opposable thumb, the recession of the jawbone and the teeth.

Yet, the same word "man," in ordinary language and among all civilized peoples, means something so totally different that it is difficult to find another word in our language with the same ambiguity. The word "man," in the second sense, signifies a set of characteristics which must be sharply distinguished from the concept "animal"—including all mammals and vertebrates. In this sense, it is as much opposed to *infusorium stentor* as to the chimpanzee, although it is obvious that man resembles the chimpanzee in his morphological, physiological and psychological characteristics much more than both man and chimpanzee resemble infusoria.

Thus, this second concept of man must have an entirely different meaning and an entirely different origin from the first, which refers only to a very small section of the vertebrate world.[1] Let us call the second concept the essential nature of man in contrast to the first concept defined within the context of natural science. The theme of this essay is to inquire whether this second concept can be justified, that is to say, whether we can assign to man unique characteristics not comparable to those of any other species.

I the stages of psychophysical life in plant, animal and man

The special place of man can be clarified only if we examine the overall structure of the biological-psychological world. I follow the stages of the development of psychic powers and capacities as science has gradually disclosed them. The limits of psychic life coincide with the boundaries of organic life itself. In addition to the phenomenologically objective qualities of living things, that they are self-moving, integrative, self-differentiating and self-limiting in a spatial and temporal sense, and so forth—I cannot discuss these matters in detail—we find as another characteristic feature that living beings are not only objects for external observers but also have a being *in and for themselves,* or an inner life of their own. It can be shown that this characteristic feature, in its structure and development, runs parallel and is intimately connected with the objective phenomena of the living process.

The lowest form of psychic life is a vital feeling, drive or impulse (*Gefühlsdrang*) devoid of consciousness, sensation and representation. It is the power behind every activity, even behind those on the highest spiritual level, and it provides the energy even for the purest acts of thought and the most tender expressions of good will. As the terms imply, "feeling" and "impulse" are not yet separated. Impulse always has a specific direction, a goal-orientation "toward something," for example, nourishment or sexual satisfaction. A bare movement "toward," as toward light, or "away from," as a state of pleasure or suffering devoid of object, are the only two modes of this primitive feeling. Yet this impulse is quite different from the centers and fields of energy that we associate with the images of inorganic bodies without consciousness. They do not have an inner life in any sense.

We must, however, attribute this first stage of psychic life to plants,* but it will not do to attribute to them, as Fechner did, sensation and consciousness. If we regard with Fechner sensation and consciousness as the most elementary aspects of psychic life—an unjustified assumption—then we must in fact deny to plants the qualities of a soul. The vital feeling of the plant is oriented toward its medium, toward the growing into this medium in accordance with certain directions like "above" and "below," toward the light or toward the earth, but only toward the undifferentiated whole of these directions. It reacts to possible resistances and realities along these general lines which are important for the life of the organism, but not to specific constituents and stimuli

* *The impression that a plant lacks an inner state arises only from the slow rate in which its living functions are performed. If observed by a speed camera this impression disappears completely.*

9

in the environment to which particular sensory qualities or primitive representations would correspond. The plant, for example, reacts specifically to the intensity of the light rays but not to particular colors and the directions of these rays. According to the findings of the Dutch Botanist Blaauw, we cannot ascribe to the plant any specific tropism, or sensation, not even the slightest semblance of a reflex arc, or associations and the conditioned reflex. For this reason, plants do not have any "sensory organs" as Haberlandt tried to show. The movements due to specific stimuli, which were previously ascribed to these organs, turned out to be component parts of the general pattern of growth in plants.

The most general concept of sensation involves a special kind of "reporting back" of a momentary physiological state, or state of motion, in the organism to a center, together with the capacity of modifying the movements that follow on the strength of this report. In the higher animals, the most primitive "sensations" would seem to be the stimuli transmitted to the brain through the ductless glands. They are the basis for sensations arising from within the organism, as well as for sensations from the outside. In the sense of this definition, the plant has no sensation and no specific "memory" beyond the dependence of its present condition upon the whole of its life history. It also has no capacity to learn in the genuine sense that we find even among the simplest infusoria. Investigations which have tried to prove that plants have conditioned reflexes and a capacity for learning seem to have been mistaken.

What is known as "instinctive life" in animals manifests itself in the plant only as a general drive toward growth and reproduction. Thus the plant shows very clearly that life is not "will to power," as Nietzsche thought, but that the essential drive of all living things is toward reproduction and death. The plant does not spontaneously choose its nourishment. It is not active in the process of fertilization; it passively fertilized through wind, birds and insects. Since it prepares its food from inorganic materials that to some extent are present everywhere, it does not need, as does the animal, to find a definite place for nourishment. Thus the plant does not have the capacity for moving in space. It does not have specific sensory experiences, nor specific instincts, nor associations, nor the conditioned reflex, nor a central nervous system. These deficiencies form a totality and must be understood in terms of the essential structure of the plant; for it can be shown that, if the plant had one of these capacities, it would have to have all the others. Since there is no sensory experience without vital impulse and without an incipient motor action, the absence of a motor system must also mean the absence of a system of sensations. The variety of sense qualities in an animal always corresponds to the varieties of its spontaneous movements. It is, in fact, a function of the latter.

The word "plant-like" or "vegetative" designates an essential orientation toward the outside. The manifold transitional phenomena between plant and animal, known to Aristotle, show that we are not dealing with empirical concepts. In the case of plants, therefore, I speak of an "ecstatic" feeling or impulse in order to indicate that they lack completely the capacity of animals to report organic states back to a center. Thus they lack completely a turning back of life upon itself, even the most primitive capacity of "reflection," or an ever-so-dim inner "conscious" state. For consciousness arises only in the primitive reflexio of sensations accompanied by an experience of resistance to an originally spontaneous movement. The plant can do without sensations only because, as the great chemist among living beings, it manufactures its own organic materials from inorganic substances. Thus its existence fulfills itself in nourishment and growth, in reproduction and death, without any specific life span for the species. Yet we find in the plant the original phenomenon of *expressiveness,* or a certain physiognomy of its inner states, such as feeble, vigorous, luxuriant or poor. "Expression" is an original phenomenon of life and not, as Darwin thought, the result of atavistic, purposive adaptation. However, plants completely lack the communicative function of animals which determines their intercourse with each other and which renders them largely independent of the immediate presence of those things that are indispensable for their survival. Only in man do the functions of expression and communication give rise to the capacity of representing and naming through signs. We do not find in the plant world the dual principle essential for all animals living in groups, the principle of pioneering and following, of setting an example and imitating.

Since the plant life lacks any centralization, especially a nervous system, the interdependence of organs and vital functions in plants is more intimate than in animals. Because of its stimulus-conducting tissue system, the plant responds to each stimulus more in terms of its total life situation than the animal. Thus it is more difficult (not easier) to explain the behavior of plants in mechanistic terms than that of animals. For it is only with the increase of the centralization of the nervous system in the animal that we find an increase in the independence of its particular reactions—and along with this, an approximation of the structure of the animal to the model of the machine.

Although incapable of adapting itself actively to the environment, whether dead or alive, the plant has teleoclitic relations both to the inorganic substances in the environment and to insects and birds, for example. Thus in a metaphysical sense, the plant—much more than the animal—may be said to be proof of the unity of life behind all morphological changes and of the gradual growth of all types of living forms in closed systems of matter and energy. The utilitarian principle, greatly overrated by both Darwinians and theists, fails completely to explain the forms and the behavior of plants, as if the plant, in an objectively teleological sense, existed "for the sake of" the animals, the animal "for the sake of" man, or as if there were a purposive striving in nature toward man. Lamarckism is equally inadequate. The rich variety of forms in the leafy parts of plants suggests, even more impressively than the forms and colors in animals, that the principle at the unknown roots of life may act in accordance with fanciful play, regulated by an aesthetic order.

The first stage of inner life, the vital feeling or drive, is present in all animals and also in man. There is no sensation, no perception, no representation behind which there is not the dark impulse burning continuously through periods of sleeping and waking. Even the simplest sensation is not merely the response to a stimulus, but always the function of a drive-motivated attention. At the same time, this impulse is the unity of all the highly differentiated drives and affects in man. According to recent findings, it may have its seat in the human brain stem, which is probably also the center of the endocrine glands whose function is to mediate between somatic and psychic events. Moreover, this vital feeling is also the subject of that primary experience of *resistance* which is the root of experiencing what is called "reality," especially the unity and the impression of "reality" which precedes any specific representation. Representations and mediated thinking (inferences) can never give us anything but this or that quality in the world. Its "reality" as such is given only in an experience of resistance accompanied by anxiety.[1]

In biological terms, the vegetative nervous system in man which, as the name implies, regulates the distribution of nourishment, shows man's affinity with the plant. The periodic withdrawal of energy away from the animal system, which regulates the outward behavior, and toward the vegetative system, is probably the basic condition for the rhythm between waking and sleeping states. In this sense, sleep is a relatively plant-like state in man.*

The second essential form in the objective stages of psychic life is what we call "instinct"—a difficult and obscure concept. We shall try to remove this obscurity by avoiding, at least to begin with, any definition in psychological terms, and by defining the concept exclusively in terms of behavior. The behavior of an organism is always open to external observation and description. It can be specified independently of the physiological processes causing it, and without introducing any physical or chemical stimuli into its characteristics. We can describe unities and changes of

* As Fechner observed, the vegetative principle seems to predominate in women and in races that till the soil in contrast to those that raise herds and are nomads, and in Asia as a whole (except for the Jewish parts). [In the original this passage occurs in the text. Trans.]

behavior under changing environmental conditions without, and prior to, any causal explanation in physiological or psychological terms. We thus gain meaningful relations which have a holistic and teleoclitic character. It is a mistake on the part of "behaviorists" to include in the concept of behavior the physiological conditions of its origin. What is valuable in the concept is precisely that it is psychophysically neutral. In other words, any mode of outward behavior is always expressing the inner state as well, for there is no inner state which does not "express" itself directly or indirectly in behavior. Thus it can and must always be explained in two respects, in both psychological and physiological terms at the same time. It is just as much a mistake to choose a psychological or a physiological explanation to the exclusion of the other. In descriptive terms, behavior is the intermediate field of observation from which we must start.

In this sense, we call behavior "instinctive" when it has the following characteristics. First, it must be meaningful, that is, it must be purposive (teleoclitic) for the whole of the living organism, its nourishment and reproduction or for the whole of another living organism. In short, it must serve its own life or that of another organism.

Secondly, it must have a definite unchanging rhythm. It is the definite rhythm that matters, not the organs which are used for the behavior and which may be exchanged in case of the loss of one or the other, nor the combinations of specific movements which may also change, depending upon the initial position of the animal. This shows the nonmechanistic nature of the instinct: it is impossible to reduce it to a combination of chains or reflexes or to "tropisms." Such a rhythm, such a pattern in time in which the parts mutually condition each other is not acquired through association, practice or habit, according to the principle which Jennings called "trial and error." The purposive movement need not refer to the present situation, but may aim at goals that are distant both in space and time. Thus, for example, an animal prepares in a meaningful, purposive way for the winter or for the laying of its eggs, even though it can be shown that as an individual it has never experienced similar situations and that any information from, or imitation of, members of the same species is ruled out. It behaves—not unlike the behavior of an electron according to quantum theory—"as if" it foresaw a future state.

The third characteristic of instinctive behavior is that it responds only to typically recurring situations which are significant for the life of the species and not for the particular experience of the individual. Instinct always serves the species, whether one's own or another species which is vitally related to one's own—hosts and parasites, the growth of galls in plants, insects and birds that fertilize plants. This characteristic distinguishes instinctive behavior, on the one hand, from self-training, from trial and error and from all learning, and, on the other, from the use of intelligence. These modes of behavior, as we shall see, serve primarily the individual and not the species. Instinctive behavior, therefore, is never a reaction to specific factors in the environment —that vary from individual to individual. It is always a reaction to a completely specific *structure,* of an environmental pattern typical for a species. Thus, while the special factors can be changed to a large extent without disturbing the instinct or leading to error, the slightest variation in structure produces confusion. This is what is meant by the "rigidity" of the instinct as distinguished from the high degree of flexibility and the behavior based on training, self-training and intelligence. In his monumental study, *Souvenirs entomologiques,* J. H. Fabre has described an impressive variety of such instinctive behavior with great precision.

Next, in line with its usefulness for the species, the instinct is innate and hereditary with respect to specific modes of behavior, and not only with respect to the general capacity of acquiring certain modes of behavior as is the case with the capacity to acquire habits or to respond to training and intelligence. Innateness, however, does not mean that what is called instinctive behavior must be present at the time of birth. It means only that it is coordinated with fixed stages of growth and maturation, and possibly even (in case of polymorphism) with different developmental stages in animals.

Finally, a very significant characteristic of instinct is that it represents a form of behavior which is independent of the number of attempts that an animal makes in order to deal with a situation. In this sense, it is "complete" from the outset. Just as the organism of the animal cannot be conceived as having come about through small differentiated steps of variation, so instinct did not develop through the accumulation of partial movements that proved successful. Instinct, to be sure, is capable of specialization through experience and learning—as may be seen in the case of hunting animals where the instinct to hunt a certain prey is inherited, but not the skill to do so successfully. But what training and experience accomplished in this case corresponds, as it were, to variations on an old melody, not to the learning of a new one. Thus, the instinct is integrated with the morphogenesis of the living organism and often operates in closest association with the physiological functions that produce the structural form of the animal body.

Very important is the relationship between instinct and sensations, or the activity of the sensory functions and organs, even memory. It is impossible that instincts are the product of sensory experience. The sensory stimulus only triggers the rhythmically definite sequence of instinctive behavior. It does not determine what this behavior is. Both olfactory and visual stimuli may trigger the same mode of behavior. Therefore, it is not necessary to have sensations of the same kind, let alone of the same quality. But the converse holds: *what an animal can imagine and perceive is controlled by the a priori relation of its instincts to the structure of the environment.* The same is true for reproducing memories. They always take place, first, within the meaningful context of dominant tasks set by the instincts (their overdetermination) and, only secondarily, as a result of the frequency of associations, conditioned reflexes and practice. An animal sees and hears what is significant for its instinctive behavior, even in the case of the same stimuli and sensory conditions. In the evolutionary perspective, all afferent nerve paths have developed only after the formation of efferent paths and effector organs. Even in man, perceiving is based upon an impulse to see or upon a more general impulse toward a waking state. Sleep cuts off all sensory organs and functions. Thus both sensory experience and memory are deeply imbedded in instinct.

The so-called "drives" or "needs" in man are the exact opposite of instinctive behavior in that, from the point of view of the whole organism, they may be completely meaningless—for example, the need for drugs. It is impossible to derive, as Loeb did, instinctive behavior from mechanically conceived tropisms. These are themselves simple instincts. It is just as impossible to reduce them to a combination of single reflexes or chain of reflexes (as in Jennings or Alverdes). There are no single reflexes according to the latest research—not even the patella reflex or the blinking reflex is a purely mechanical reflex. Finally, it is impossible to reduce an instinct to the inheritance of characteristics acquired through habit and self training (as we find in Spencer), that is, ultimately to laws of association and conditioned reflex. It is just as impossible to envisage instinct (as Wundt did) as the automatic response of what was originally an "intelligent" mode of behavior. The instinct is always a part of the growth of the species itself; in pure strains it does not change at all. Partial modifications through habit and training do not change the instinct any more than they change the organic structure of an animal.

Instinct is without doubt a more primitive form of psychic life than the complexes formed through association. We can show that the psychic processes determined by the loss of association or habit are localized considerably higher in the nervous system than are instinctive modes of behavior. Precisely those modes of behavior that form a meaningful unit—the grasping of an object or the singing of a melody— may still be possible under pathological conditions, when less unified and less meaningful modes, such as the specific movement of the single finger or the singing of scales, can no longer be performed. The fixed structure of meaningful, behavioral complexes is, on the whole conditioned subcortically. The cerebral cortex is essentially an organ of dissociation, not of association, as compared with the more unified and more deeply localized modes of behavior.

We may say that, genetically, there are two primitive developments of instinctive behavior—or two products of "disintegration" in a nonpejorative sense. There is, on the one hand, the emergence of relatively simple sensations and ideas from diffuse complexes, and the associative connection between them, or the emergence of a single "drive" demanding satisfaction out of an instinctive, purposive complex. There are, on the other hand, the beginnings of intelligence which tries to put some "artificial" meaning back into the now meaningless automatic responses. Both developments coincide with each other and with the emergence of the individual from bondage to the species. They also make possible the variety of particular and unique situations which may confront the individual.

Thus creative dissociation, not association or the synthesis of single pieces, is the basic process of psychic evolution. The same is true in physiological terms. The more simple its physiological organization, the less does an organism resemble a mechanism. Yet, it develops—up to the approach of death and the cytomorphism of its organs—what resembles more and more a mechanical structure and mechanical modes of behavior. It can probably be shown that intelligence is not, as Karl Bühler thinks, added to the associative mental processes (or the conditioned reflex) at a higher stage of life, but develops strictly uniform and parallel with associative processes. It is, as Alverdes and Buytendyk have shown, by no means present only in the highest mammals but even in infusoria. It is as if what in the instinct is purposive, but inflexible and fixed to the species, is made flexible in individuals through intelligence, and as if what is automatic in the instinct is made mechanical and relatively nonpurposive in association and the conditioned reflex, yet, at the same time, is also capable of more varied combinations. This helps us to understand why the arthropoda which morphologically have a different and more rigid structure than higher animals also have the most complete set of instincts, but hardly show any sign of intelligent behavior. Man, on the other hand, as a more flexible type of mammal in whom intelligence and associative memory are most highly developed, has instincts that are poorly developed or arrested.

If we interpret instinctive behavior in physiological terms it represents an individual unity of foreknowledge and action so that there is never *more* knowledge than what is involved in the next stage of the action. There is, to be sure, the beginning of the separation between sensation and reaction (reflex arc), but there is still the closest possible connection of both in terms of function. Moreover, knowledge inherent in the instinct is not a knowledge by means of representations, images or even ideas. It is rather a feeling of value-charged resistances which are differentiated as attractive or repulsive according to these value impressions. It makes no sense to talk as Reimarus did, about innate "representations" in the case of instincts. As compared with the vital impulse, instinct is concerned with points of the environment which, though frequently repeated, are yet specific and different in content, and which must be perceived. Thus it represents an increasing specialization of the vital drive and its qualities.

Of the two modes of behavior—the "habitual" and the "intelligent"—both of which arise out of instinct, the habitual mode of behavior is the third form of psychic life. It represents the phenomena of association, reproduction and conditioned reflex: in short, the capacity which we call "associative memory." This capacity does not go with all living beings; plants do not have it, as Aristotle saw correctly. We must attribute it to all living organisms whose behavior is modified slowly and continually on the basis of earlier behavior with respect to a purposive and useful end. Moreover, progress in this direction depends strictly upon the number of attempts or trial movements. The fact that an animal spontaneously makes such trial movements (even spontaneous play among young dogs and horses is included here) and the fact that it tends to repeat these movements regardless of whether they result in pleasure or pain have nothing to do with memory, but are the prerequisite for all reproduction and point to an innate drive toward repetition. But the fact that an animal later tends to repeat those movements that were successful in producing positive satisfactions (instead of those which were not successful), so that the former become "fixed," is the basic fact behind the principle of trial and error. Wherever we find such facts, we speak of "training" when it is merely a quantitative matter or of "habit" when it is a qualitative matter, and depending upon whether man intervenes or not, of self-training or conditioned training.

To attribute this psychic or physiological capacity to all living organisms is justified only in the sense that the behavior of living things is never a product merely of the immediately preceding state, but always involves the entire prehistory of the organism. It is, however, false to say that, in the case of all living beings, specific sensory and motor modes of behavior facilitate the later appearance of similar behavior. For plant life, as we have shown, does not have this capacity, and cannot have it, because it lacks the capacity of reporting organic states back to a central agency or motor system. The basis of all associative memory is what Pavlov called the conditioned reflex. The dog, for example, not only secretes gastric juices when food enters its stomach but as soon as it sees the food or hears the steps of the man who ordinarily brings the food. Man even secretes gastric juices when it is suggested to him in his sleep that he is taking nourishment. If one repeatedly sounds a signal simultaneously with behavior produced by a special stimulus, the same behavior can also be produced by means of the signal without the appropriate stimulus. This is called conditioned reflex.

In the context of psychic life, its only analogy is the so-called law of association, according to which there is a tendency to reproduce the entire complex of representations or to restore its missing links when we experience a part of this complex in either a sensory or a motor context. If a complex breaks into separate pieces, these pieces may also be combined again according to the law of "contiguity and similarity." The so-called laws of association result therefrom. No doubt these represent peculiar laws of psychic life which play a great role among the higher animals, especially among vertebrates and mammals; yet there is no doubt that we never find a completely rigid association of single ideas based only upon the law of contiguity and similarity, that is to say, upon the partial identity of the incipient ideas with earlier complexes. This happens no more than the occurrence of a completely isolated and constantly uniform reflex in a separate and locally defined organ, or no more than the occurrence of a "pure" perception strictly proportionate to its stimulus and independent of the varying drive attitudes and all memory content. (Every perception is always a function of the stimulus *and* of drive-motivated attention.)

Just as there is no "pure" perception, so there is no "pure" association. All associative memory is subject to the power of drives, needs and the tasks set by these needs or the demands of the trainer. Laws of association, therefore, as the laws of physics that deal with general processes, only describe statistical regularities. They are not the basic laws of mental life as Locke, Hume, Mill and other psychologists of association believed. Concepts like "pure" sensation or "associative reflex" are in the nature of *limiting concepts,* indicating the direction of certain types of changes, whether psychic or physiological. Approximately pure associations are probably found only in connection with a definite suspension or loss of intellectual controls, as in the case of associating sounds of spoken words without meaning (flight of ideas). Genetically, this is not an original phenomenon. Only in old age when the drives diminish in strength and differentiation do the psychic processes approximate the associative model as the changes in writing, drawing, painting and speaking in very old people seem to indicate. They assume an increasingly additive, nonholistic character. In other words, the laws of association hold approximately for an organism in a state of senility. Again, in old age sensation is more closely proportionate to the stimulus; it approximates the "pure" sensation.

Even as the physical organism in the course of life becomes, relatively speaking, more and more a mechanism—until it succumbs completely to such a condition in death—

so our psychic life, too, produces more and more purely habitual connections between ideas and modes of behavior. In old age man becomes more and more a slave of habit. And even as the sober perception of states of affairs without surplus of fantasy and without mythical treatment is a late phenomenon in the life of the individual and groups—the early life of man, as well as the psychic life of a child, is overgrown with the spontaneous creation of a fantasy world of drives and wishes—so associative memory, localized in the higher regions of the cortex, is a late phenomenon.[2] It is not an original phenomenon to which later are added synthetic functions by means of "relational thinking" or an "oversoul." Nor is associative memory "pure" in the sense that it is ever completely devoid of intellectual influence. It never happens that the trend from associative chance reactions to meaningful reactions is strictly proportionate to the number of trials. The curves show discontinuities in this respect: the transition from random to meaningful connections occurs sooner than expected, according to the laws of probability operating behind the principle of trial and error. It is as if something like "insight" comes into play with the number of trials.

The principle of associative memory is at work in all animals and is a consequence of the emergence of the reflex arc, the separation of the sensory from the motor system. There are great differences in its distribution. The typically "instinct animals" (arthopoda) with a closed, chainlike system show it least. It is most prevalent among animals (vertebrates and mammals) with a more flexible and less rigid structure and with a greater capacity for combining partial movements into new or more developed movements. In man the principle of association and reproduction extends farthest.

From the moment of its first appearance, this principle is connected with the attempt to imitate actions and movements transmitted by members of the same species through affects and signals. "Imitating" and "copying" are but special manifestations of the repetition drive (now applied to the behavior of others) which was originally applied to its own modes of behavior and experience and which is the energy, as it were, behind reproductive memory.

The combination of both phenomena is responsible for the important concept of tradition. Tradition, in this sense, adds a completely new dimension to biological inheritance linking animal behavior with the past life of the species. It must be sharply distinguished from all conscious memory and from all cultural inheritance by means of symbols, sources and documents, that is, from all historical knowledge. The latter is characteristic of man only, yet tradition is present already among herds and packs and other social forms of animal life. Here, too, the herd "learns" from the example set by the pioneers and passes its knowledge on to coming generations.

Tradition, therefore, makes possible a certain kind of "progress." Yet human evolution, in the true sense, depends upon a progressive decomposition of tradition. Conscious memory of an individual, unique event, and the constant identification of a plurality of memories as constituting one and the same past, are possible only for man. It is a process which invariably contributes to the dissolution, yes, the actual death, of a living tradition. Traditional contents are always given as "present," "without a date"; they operate in our present activities without becoming objectified in a definite temporal distance. In tradition, the past influences more by suggestion than by knowledge.* The reduction of the power of tradition is a continuous process in human history. It is an achievement of human reason which, in one and the same act, *objectifies* the content of the tradition, thus throwing it back, as it were, into the past where it belongs and, at the same time, clearing the ground for new discoveries and inventions in the present. A gradual weakening of those powers which "make habit the nursemaid of mankind" is an essential part of all history. The pressure which tradition continually exerts upon our behavior, on a preconscious level, is continuously reduced by the advances made in the historical sciences.

The operation of the associative principle means both emerges more and more from bondage to the species and the increase of centralization and the concomitant mechanization of organic life. It means, further, that the individual emerges more and more from bondage to the species and from the nonadaptive rigidity of instinct. For only with the operation of this principle can the individual adapt himself to new situations, to situations not typical of the species. Thus the individual ceases to be no more than a point of transition in the reproductive process of the species. If the principle of association, as compared with practical intelligence is, as we shall see, still the principle of rigidity and

* *Suggestion, according to Schilder, probably hypnosis as well, is a common phenomenon in the animal world. Hypnosis may have emerged as an auxiliary function in mating and probably originally served the purpose of putting the female in a state of lethargy. Suggestion is a primary phenomenon as opposed to communication; for example, communicating a proposition the meaning and factual reference of which is grasped by "understanding." This capacity to grasp the intended factual reference expressed in a spoken sentence is found only in man.*

habit—a "conservative principle," as it were—it is a powerful instrument of liberation in relation to instinctive behavior.
It creates an entirely new dimension of possibilities for the
enrichment of life.

This is also true for drives, feelings and affects. The
instinct that is liberated from its fate appears, to a certain
extent, among the higher animals and, at the same time,
opens up an horizon of excess. It becomes a potent source
of pleasure independent of the needs and necessities of life as
a whole. The sexual drive, for example, is an incorruptible
servant of life only as long as it is imbedded in the deep
rhythm of the rutting season. Once freed from this instinctive rhythm, it becomes more and more an autonomous
source of pleasure. Thus, in the higher animals, especially
in domesticated animals, it can far outgrow the purpose of
life; for example, onanism in monkeys and dogs. The drives
originally aim at modes of behavior and goods in the world,
and not at pleasure as a feeling. If they are used by man
primarily as a source of pleasure, as in hedonism, we are
dealing with a late and decadent phenomenon of life.[3] A
way of life aiming exclusively at pleasure is decidedly a manifestation of aging, in the life of the individual and the race,
as shown in the case of the old drinker who "savors each
drop" and analogous phenomena in the erotic life. It is also
a sign of aging when the enjoyment of the higher or lower
psychic functions is divorced from the state of pleasure accompanying the gratification of drives, or when the state of
pleasure outweighs the enjoyment of vital and spiritual functions. The "pleasure principle," therefore, is not an original
phenomenon, as hedonism believes, but a consequence of an
intensified associative intelligence. Only in man does the

capacity to isolate the drive from instinctive behavior and to separate the state of pleasure from functional enjoyment assume such monstrous forms that it is quite correct to say, man can be either more or less than an animal, but never *an animal*.

Wherever nature has produced this new psychic form of associative memory it has also, as I suggested, built into the beginnings of this capacity a corrective for its dangers. This corrective is none other than the fourth essential form of psychic life—practical intelligence. Closely connected with it and also still rooted in the organism is the capacity to choose in action, or the capacity to choose among material goods and among members of the same species in the reproductive process. (This is the beginning of Eros.) [4]

Again, we can define intelligent behavior without reference to psychic processes. An organism behaves "intelligently" when it satisfies the following conditions: It must be capable of responding, without trial and error, to a new situation meaningfully, "cleverly" or "foolishly"; that is, aiming at a goal but missing it, for only one who is intelligent can be foolish. It must be capable of solving the drive-determined problem suddenly and, above all, independently of the number of previous attempts. We say that this intelligence is rooted in the organism as long as the behavior serves the drive or the satisfaction of a need. We call this intelligence "practical" because it always aims at some action by means of which the organism obtains or misses a goal set by its drives. In man the same intelligence can be put in the service of purely *spiritual* goals; only then it is raised above cleverness, prudence and cunning.

On the psychological side, we can define intelligence as a sudden insight into a connected context of facts and values within the environment that is not perceived directly now nor was ever perceived previously so that it is a function of reproduction. In positive terms, intelligence is insight into a state of affairs on the basis of a structure of relations whose basic elements are partly given in experience, partly completed in anticipatory representation, as for example, in the case of certain visual intuitions. Anticipation, therefore, is always characteristic of this type of thinking which is productive, not reproductive. It is a kind of prevision of a new state of affairs never experienced before (*pro-videntia, prudentia,* cleverness, cunning).

The difference between intelligence and associative memory is obvious: the situation to be grasped and to be mastered is not only new and atypical for the species, but above all new for the individual. Such an objectively meaningful behavior takes place suddenly and prior to new trials, and independent of the number of previous trials. The suddenness of the experience is reflected in expression, for example, when the eyes of the animal light up, an expression which Wolfgang Köhler aptly called an "Aha" experience. Moreover, it is not the combination of experiences (given simultaneously and in part identical or similar) that provide the solution to the problem. Nor do fixed and typically recurring configurations in the environment elicit intelligent behavior. It is, rather, the objective relations in the environment determined and selected, as it were, in accordance with the role of the drive which produce the new idea: relations such as equal, similar, analogous, intervening, instrumental function or cause.

Whether animals, especially the highest apes, such as chimpanzees, have reached this stage of psychic life is much discussed in the literature. I can only make a few cursory comments on this subject. The controversy has not ceased since W. Köhler published his experiments with chimpanzees, conducted with great patience, precision and ingenuity at the experimental station at Tenerife.[5] In my opinion, Köhler is completely justified in attributing to his experimental animals simple intelligent behavior, as defined above. Others dispute this: nearly everyone tries to defend, with different arguments, the old doctrine according to which animals have nothing but associative memory and instinct, and according to which intelligence (even as a primitive inference without symbols) is a monopoly of man.

Köhler's experiments were conducted as follows: Between the animal and its goal-object (a fruit, usually a banana) were interposed complicated detours, obstacles or objects that could serve as "instruments"—for example, boxes, ropes, sticks, even sticks that had to be fitted together, procured or made. It was then observed if, how and by what (presumably) mental capacities the animal knew how to achieve its goal, and what were the fixed limits in its performance. The experiments, in my judgment, clearly prove that the achievements of these animals cannot all be explained in terms of instinct and associative processes (memory components) accompanying them. In some cases, we have genuine acts of intelligence.

I shall briefly sketch what seems to me to be involved in this kind of practical intelligence. As the goal-object—say, a fruit—lights up in the visual field of the animal and is set off, as an independent entity, the surrounding visual field and all of the objects in the environment are peculiarly restructured, especially the visual field between the animal and fruit. It is restructured in its objective relations. It is thrown into a relatively "abstract" perspective so that objects which, perceived by themselves, are either indifferent to the animal or have characteristics such as "something to bite into," or "something to play with," or "something to sleep on" assume the abstract dynamic characteristic of "something to get the fruit with"—for example, a blanket which the animal fetches from his sleeping quarters in order to bring within reach the fruit lying outside the cage. Moreover, it is not only objects like actual sticks similar to branches on which fruits might hang in the normal arboreal habitat of the animal which are used for this purpose. This might still be attributed to instinct. It may also be a piece of wire, pieces of straw, the brim of a straw hat or a blanket—anything that satisfies the abstract representation of "movable and elongated." It is the dynamic energy of the drive itself that is here objectified and projected into constituents of the environment. The object used by the animal acquires (only in this case, to be sure) the dynamic functional value of an "instrument," an "object for bringing the fruit nearer." It acquires the characteristic of being focused upon the goal in the visual field: The rope or the stick itself seems to point to the goal, if not actually to move toward it.

Perceptual experiences in animals (in children and primitive peoples as well) are much more receptive to impulses, drives and wishes. Thus it is not impossible to imagine that the displacement of the drive onto the thing-world of the environment (as if the things themselves were driven toward the fruit, not only the animal) should also bring about changes in the perceptual field which make the stick "move" toward the fruit—a phenomenon which E. R. Jaensch has shown in the case of perceptual images in children. Here we catch the first glimpse of the phenomenon of causality or efficacy which cannot be explained, as Hume did, in terms of the regular sequence and succession of events. On the contrary, it is a dynamic phenomenon, based upon objectifying the causality experienced in the drive-motivated action and coincides, in this case, completely with its "instrumental" function. In the animal, of course, the restructuring of the field which we have been describing does not take place through conscious, reflective activity, but rather through a kind of intuitive, objective replacing of the things in the environment. Nevertheless, it is an act of genuine intelligence and discovery, not an act of instinct or habit. The great differences that animals exhibit with regard to this kind of behavior confirm that it is an expression of intelligence, not instinct.

The same applies to choice, and action based on choice. It is a mistake to deny that animals have the capacity to choose and to suppose that they are always moved by the stronger impulse. The animal is not a mechanism of drives, just as it is not a mechanism of instinct, associations and conditioned reflexes. In the first place, the system of drives is highly differentiated: it consists of dominant drives, and executive, subordinate and auxiliary drives; again, of drives concerned with the performance of general and specific tasks. In the second place, the animal has a drive center corresponding to the unified structure of its nervous system. It is capable of intervening spontaneously in its constellation of drives from this central organization so that, to a certain extent at least, it can avoid immediate gratifications in order to obtain greater gratifications that are more distant in time and may involve a circuitous route. Yet, the animal definitely lacks the capacity to choose between values as such—for example, the capacity to prefer the useful to the pleasant as a value in itself independent of the concrete material goods and the accompanying "disposition." [6] In its affects the animals is still much closer to man than in its intelligence. We find in animals the capacity for generosity, help, reconciliation, friendship and similar phenomena.

II *the essence of*
spirit

We have now come to the problem that is crucial for our inquiry. If the animal has intelligence, does this mean there is only a difference in degree between man and animal —or is there still an essential difference? Is there still in man, beyond the stages of life discussed heretofore, something that is quite different and unique, something that is not yet defined by, or included in, the capacity for choice and intelligence?

Here the paths divide sharply. One side would reserve intelligence and choice for man and deny them to the animal. This view, in fact, affirms that there is an essential, qualitative difference, but locates it at a point where in my opinion it does not exist. The other side, especially the evolutionists of the Darwinian-Lamarckian school, deny that there is an essential difference between man and animal precisely because the animal does have intelligence. These writers adhere, in one way or another, to a unified conception of man which I have called the theory of *"Homo faber."* Accordingly, they do not recognize any distinctive metaphysical or ontological status of man.

For my own part, I reject both views. I assert that the

nature of man, or that which may be called his unique place in nature, goes far beyond the capacity for choice and intelligence and would not be reached even if we were to enlarge these powers, in a quantitative sense, to infinity.* But it would also be a mistake to think that the new element which gives man his unique characteristics is nothing but a new essential form of being added to the previous stages of psychic life—the vital impulse, instinct, associative memory, intelligence and choice; in other words, an element which still belongs to the psychic and vital functions and capacities, and which falls into the province of psychology and biology.

The new principle transcends what we call "life" in the most general sense. It is not a stage of life, especially not a stage of the particular mode of life called psyche, but a principle opposed to life as such, even to life in man. Thus it is a genuinely new phenomenon which cannot be derived from the natural evolution of life, but which, if reducible to anything, leads back to the ultimate Ground of Being of which "life" is a particular manifestation.

The Greeks affirmed the existence of such a principle and called it reason.[1] We will use a more inclusive term and call it "spirit"—a term which includes the concept of reason, but which, in addition to conceptual thought, also includes the intuition of essences and a class of voluntary and emotional acts such as kindness, love, remorse, reverence, wonder, bliss, despair and free decision. The center of action in which spirit appears within a finite mode of being we call "person" in sharp contrast to all functional vital centers

* Between the clever chimpanzee and an Edison, taking the latter only as a technician, there is only a difference in degree—though a great one to be sure.

which, from an inner perspective, may be called "psychic centers."

What, then, is this spirit, this new crucial principle? Seldom has a word been more abused so that it hardly has a clear meaning for anybody. If we put at the head of this concept of spirit a special function of knowledge which it alone can provide, then the essential characteristic of the spiritual being, regardless of its psychological make-up, is its existential liberation from the organic world—its freedom and detachability from the bondage and pressure of life, from its dependence upon all that belongs to life, including its own drive-motivated intelligence.

The spiritual being, then, is no longer subject to its drives and its environment. Instead, it is "free from the environment" or, as we shall say, "open to the world." Such a being has a "world." Moreover, such a being is capable of transforming the primary centers of resistance and reaction into "objects." (The animal remains immersed in them "ecstatically.") Such a being is capable of grasping the qualities of objects without the restriction imposed upon this thing-world by the system of vital drives and the mediating functions and organs of the sensory apparatus.

Thus, spirit is objectivity, or the determination of the objective nature of things. Spirit only belongs to a being capable of strict objectivity. More precisely: in order to be a bearer of spirit, the being must have *reversed*, dynamically and in principle, its relationship both to external reality and to itself as compared with the animal, including its intelligence. What is this reversal?

In the case of the animal, whether it is highly organized or not, every action and reaction, even that which is "intelligent," proceeds from a physiological condition of the nervous system with which are coordinated, on the psychic side, certain instincts, drives and sensory perceptions. What does not interest the instinct or drive is not given. What is given is given only as a center of resistance to attraction and repulsion, that is, to the animal as a biological unit. Thus the impetus from a physiological-psychological condition is always the first act in the drama of an animal's behavior toward the environment. The structure of the environment is precisely adapted to the physiological peculiarities of the animal, and indirectly to its morphological characteristics as well, and to its instincts and sensory structure, which form a strictly functional unity. Animals only notice and grasp those things which fall into the secure boundaries of their environmental structure. The second act of the drama of animal behavior consists in making some actual changes in the environment as a result of the animal's free action with respect to a dominant goal set by its drives. The third act consists in a concomitant change of its physiological-psychological condition. The course of animal behavior therefore always has this form:

$$A \text{ (animal)} \rightleftharpoons E \text{ (environment)}$$

The situation is altogether different in the case of a being that has spirit. Such a being is capable of behavior (at least in so far as it makes use of spirit) that runs a diametrically opposed course. The first act of this new and human drama is this: Its behavior is "motivated" by a complex of sensations and ideas raised to the status of an object. It is, in principle, independent of the drives and the sensuous surfaces in the environment conditioned by the system of drives

38

that appear in the visual and auditory fields. The second act of the drama consists in the voluntary inhibition, or release, of a drive and of the corresponding reaction. The third act consists of a final and intrinsic change with regard to the objective nature of a thing. The course of such behavior is "world-openness," and such behavior, once it appears, is capable of unlimited expansion—as far as the "world" of existing things extends.

$$M \ (man) \ \rightleftharpoons \ W \ (world) \longrightarrow \longrightarrow$$

Man, then, is a being that can exhibit, to an unlimited degree, behavior which is open to the world. To become human is to acquire this openness to the world by virtue of the spirit.

The animal has no "object." It lives, as it were, ecstatically immersed in its environment which it carries along as a snail carries its shell. It cannot transform the environment into an object. It cannot perform the peculiar act of detachment and distance by which man transforms an "environment" into the "world," or into a symbol of the world. It cannot perform the act by which man transforms the centers of resistance determined by drives and affects into "objects."

Objective being or objectification, therefore, is the most formal category of the logical aspect of spirit. I might say the animal is involved too deeply in the actualities of life which correspond to its organic needs and conditions ever to experience and grasp them as objects. The animal, to be sure, no longer lives in quite the same ecstatic state as the plant does, that is to say, subject to nothing but the vital impulse without sensation, representation, consciousness, and without any reporting back of the particular states of the organism to an inner center. Owing to the separation of the sensory and the motor system, and owing to its continuously holding back of specific sensory contents, the animal, as it were, owns itself. It does have a "body schema." But in relation to the environment, the animal still behaves "ecstatically"—even when it acts "intelligently." Its intelligence remains strictly within the bounds of organic drives and practical needs. The spiritual act in man, in contrast to the simple reporting back of the animal's body schema and its contents, is essentially linked with the second dimension stage of the reflexive act. We call this act "concentration," and if we bring the act together with the goal at which concentration aims, we have "self-consciousness," by which is meant the consciousness that the spiritual center of action has of itself. The animal has consciousness as distinguished from the plant, but, as Leibniz knew, it has no self-consciousness. It does not "own itself," it is not its own master; hence, it is not conscious of itself.

Concentration, self-consciousness and the capacity to objectify the original centers of resistance encountered by the drives—these characteristics form a single indivisible structure which, as such, is peculiar only to man. Self-consciousness, or the new act of centering its existence, is the second essential characteristic of man. By virtue of the spirit, man is capable of expanding the environment into the dimension of a world and of objectifying resistance. He is also capable —and this is most remarkable—of objectifying his own physiological and psychological states, every psychic experience and every vital function. It is for this reason that this being can also throw his life away freely.

The animal hears and sees—without knowing that it

does so. The psyche of the animal functions and works, but the animal is not a potential psychologist or physiologist. We must single out very exceptional ecstatic states in man; for example, the state of emerging from hypnosis or the state induced by drugs—techniques that in certain cases, as in orgiastic cults of all kinds, render the spirit inactive—in order to imagine the normal condition of the animal. The animal does not even experience its drives as its own, but as dynamic pushes and pulls that emanate from the things in the environment. Primitive man, who in certain psychic characteristics is still close to the animal, does not say, "I avoid this thing," but "This thing is taboo." For the animal there are only those factors in the environment that are determined by attraction and repulsion. The monkey who jumps hither and yonder lives, as it were, in successive states of ecstasy (comparable to the pathological flights of ideas in man). It does not have a "will" that outlasts the drives and their changing states, and that preserves a kind of continuity in the variations of the psychophysical conditions. An animal always arrives, as it were, elsewhere than at the destination at which it originally aimed. Nietzsche made a profound and correct remark when he said, "Man is an animal that can make promises."

There are four essential stages in which all existence manifests itself with regard to inner being. *Inorganic* forms have no such inner state or self-being whatsoever. They have no center that is their own; hence, no medium, no environment in which they live. What we designate as unities in this world, down to the world of molecules, atoms and electrons depends entirely upon our power to divide bodies, whether we do so in actual practice or in conceptual thought.

Every inorganic body is a unity only within a specific context of causal action relative to other bodies. The nonspatial centers of energy, which give the appearance of extension through time and which we attribute to the images of bodies on metaphysical grounds, are mutually interacting points of energy in which the lines of an energy field run together.

An organism, on the other hand, is always an ontic center. It invariably forms "its own" spatiotemporal unity and individuality. These are not produced, as in the case of inorganic unities, by virtue of our capacity to synthesize, which is itself conditioned biologically. An organism is self-limiting. It has individuality. To dissect it means to murder it, that is, to destroy its essence and being. To the vital impulse of the plant there corresponds a center and a medium into which the plant, relatively open in its growth, is placed without any reporting back of its varying states to its center. Yet the plant does have an "inner being" or a kind of soul. In the animal, however, we find both sensation and consciousness and, together with them, a central organization for the reporting back of changing conditions in the organism and the capacity of modifying the central organization on the basis of these reports. It is thus given to itself a second time. Man, however, by virtue of his spirit, is given to himself a third time: in self-consciousness and in the capacity to objectify psychic states and his sensory and motor system. "Person," as applied to man, therefore, must be envisaged as the center of acts raised beyond the interaction and contrast be-between organism and environment. Does this hierarchy of forms not appear as if there were different levels in the structure of being in which the ultimate Ground of Being bends back more and more upon itself to become more and more conscious of itself on higher levels and new dimensions—until it comes to possess and grasp itself completely in man?

The structure of man—his self-consciousness and his capacity to objectify both the environment and his own physiological and psychic states and the causal relations existing in both—helps to explain a number of specific human characteristics. I shall mention a few of them.

Only in man do we find the fully developed categories of thing and substance. The animal does not have them. The spider waiting for prey will rush immediately after an insect that is caught in its web and whose presence is probably communicated through the tactile sense by a faint pull. But if the insect is put into such proximity that the spider can see it, the spider will run away. Thus the thing that is seen is quite different from the thing that is felt by touch. The spider is incapable of coordinating visual space with kinaesthetic space, or the respective objects disclosed in each. Even the highest animals do not have a fully developed thing-category. The ape that is handed a half-peeled banana will again run away from it, whereas he will eat it if it is completely peeled, and he will peel and eat it if it is not peeled at all. The thing called "banana" has not changed for the animal; rather, the thing has changed into something else. The animal lacks a center which would relate all the psychophysical functions of seeing, hearing, smelling and grasping, and the different things coordinated with them, into a unity belonging to one and the same concrete object.

Next, man has, from the start, a unified space. For example, a person born blind whose sight is restored through an operation does not learn to synthesize different spaces—

such as tactile space, visual space, auditory space, and kin-aesthetic space—into a unified intuition of space. What he learns is only how to identify sensory data as symbols and qualities of the same thing occupying one place. The animal again lacks the central function which provides a unified space as a fixed form prior to the particular things and their perception in it. More importantly, it lacks the capacity of self-reference to a center by means of which man combines all sensory data, and the drives coordinated with them, and relates them to a single world as an ordered field composed of different substances. The animal lacks a "world space" which persists as a stable background independent of the animal's movements. It also lacks the empty forms of space and time into which man is placed and in which he originally encounters things and events. These forms are possible only for a being in whom the frustration of drives always exceeds their gratification. For "empty" means, to begin with, an expectation that is not satisfied. The original "emptiness" is, as it were, the emptiness of our hearts.

The basis for the human intuitions of space and time preceding all external sensations is the capacity for spontaneous movement and action according to a definite order. The fact (apparent in certain pathological deficiencies) that tactile space is not directly coordinated with visual space, but that this coordination is possible only through the mediation of kinaesthetic sensations, also indicates that the empty form of space, at least in the sense of an unformed "spatiality," is experienced prior to any conscious sensations. In other words, it is first experienced merely on the basis of motor impulses and the capacity to produce such impulses, for it is these very motor impulses that are followed by kinaesthetic sensations. This primitive "movement-space," this "consciousness-of-being-around-and/or-surrounded," remains with us even when visual space in which the uniform manifold of extension is given, is completely removed.

Although the higher animals do have spatial manifolds (in the most primitive animals we probably find only temporal impressions) these spaces are not homogeneous. There is no fixed, prior ordering system of places in the visual sphere from which the qualities and movements of things in the environment are sharply separated. Only the highest visual organization in man (with erect posture!) has such a system, but he can lose it in pathological cases so that only the primitive space remains. The animal can no more separate the empty forms of space and time from specific objects in the environment than it can isolate the concept of "number" from the notion of plurality, the notion of more or less inherent in the things outside. It lives wholly in the concrete actuality of its immediate present. Only in man do we find the strange phenomenon that both spatial and temporal emptiness appears prior to, and is the basis of, all possible perceptions in the world of objects. This is possible only because the drive expectations converted into motor impulses outweigh the actual gratification of drives in sensation. Thus, without suspecting it, man takes his own emptiness of heart for the "infinite emptiness" of space and time—as if the latter could exist without objects. Science has corrected the serious illusion of the natural world view only very late by showing that space and time are nothing but forms of ordering things, possibilities for relations and successions among things, and that they have no independent reality apart from these things.

The animal, as I said, has no world space. A dog may have lived for years in a garden, and may have frequently visited every place in it, yet he will not be able to form an over-all picture of the garden, no matter how large or small it may be, or of the arrangements of the trees and bushes independent of his own position. He has only "environmental spaces" that vary with his movements, and he is not able to coordinate these with the garden space that is independent of the position of his own body. The reason is that he cannot objectify his own body and its movements so as to include them as variable features in his intuition of space and to reckon instinctively, as it were, with the accident of his own position as man is able to do even without science.

This achievement is but the beginning of what man continues in science. For the greatness of science is this: by means of science, man learns to reckon on a more and more comprehensive scale with his own accidental position in the universe, and with himself or his whole physical and psychical apparatus, as if it were an external object linked in strict causal relations with other things. In this way, he gradually constructs a picture of the world, the objects and laws of which are completely independent of his own psychophysical organism, of his senses, their thresholds, of his needs and their interests in things. Thus the objective world and its laws remain constant throughout the changing conditions of man's place in the universe.[2]

Man alone—in so far as he is a person—is able to go beyond himself as an organism and to transform, from a center beyond the spatiotemporal world, everything (himself included) into an object of knowledge. Thus man as a spiritual being is a being that surpasses himself in the world.

As such he is also capable of irony and humor which always indicate the transcendence of actual existence (*Dasein*). The center, however, from which man performs the acts by means of which he objectifies body, psyche and world in its spatial and temporal abundance cannot itself be part of this world. It cannot be located in space or in time: it can only be located in the highest Ground of Being itself. In his profound theory of the transcendental apperception, Kant clarified this new unity of the *cogito* as the "condition of all possible experience and, therefore, also of all objects in experience," both outer and inner, by which our own inner life becomes accessible to us. He was thus the first to raise "spirit" above "psyche" and expressly denied that spirit was nothing but a group of functions belonging to a so-called mental substance, or soul, which owes its fictitious status merely to an unjustified reification of the actual unity of the spirit.

Thus, we have come to a third important characteristic of spirit. Spirit is the only being incapable of becoming an object. It is pure actuality. It has its being only in and through the execution of its acts. The center of spirit, the person, is not an object or a substantial kind of being, but a continuously self-executing, ordered structure of acts. The person is only in and through his acts. The psychic act is not self-contained. It is an event "in" time which, in principle, we can observe from the center of spirit and which we can objectify through introspection. Psychic acts are capable of objectification, but not the spiritual act—the intentionality itself which makes the psychic process visible. We can only "collect" ourselves with regard to our being as a person: we can concentrate upon it; we cannot objectify it. Other people, too, as *persons* cannot become objects. (In this sense

47

Goethe said of Lili Schönemann that he "loved her too much" to be able to "observe" her.) We can come to "know" them only by participating in, or by entering into, their free acts, through the kind of "understanding" possible in an attitude of empathetic love, the very opposite of objectification—in short, by "identifying," as we say, with the will and love of another person and thereby with himself.

In the acts of a superindividual spirit, too, we can participate only by some kind of identification. We postulate such a spirit on the basis of the essential bond between fact and idea in so far as we assume that there is a self-realizing order of ideas independent of human consciousness, and in so far as we ascribe this order to the ultimate Ground of Being as one of its attributes. We participate in such an order in three respects: in an order of essences, in so far as the spirit is intellect; in an objective order of values in so far as the spirit expresses itself in love and in a teleological order of the world in so far as the spirit expresses itself in action. The traditional type of philosophical idealism, prevailing since St. Augustine, held that "ideas were prior to things" (*ideae ante res*), that there was providence and a *plan* of creation before the *act* of creation. But ideas do not exist "before," "in" or "after" things, but *with* them. They are created by the eternal spirit in the act of continuous world-realization (*creatio continua*). Therefore our own participation in these acts is not simply a matter of discovering or of disclosing some being or essence that exists independently of us. It is, rather, a genuine co-creation of the essences, ideas, values and goals coordinated with the eternal logos, the eternal love and the eternal will.

If we wish to clarify the special and unique quality of what we call "spirit," it is best to begin with a special spiritual act—the act of ideation. This is an act completely different from all technical intelligence and from the inferential kind of thinking, the beginnings of which we find in animals. Practical intelligence would set itself a problem such as this: I now have a pain in my arm. What caused it? How can it be removed? This would be a task for such sciences as physiology, psychology or medicine. But I can also take the same experience in a more detached and contemplative attitude, as a "case" disclosing the strange and surprising essential condition that this world is polluted by pain, evil and sorrow. Then I would ask another question: What is "pain itself" apart from the fact that I experience it here and now? What must be the nature of things that such a thing as "pain itself" is possible?

A striking example of such an act of ideation is the well-known conversion of the Buddha. The prince encounters one poor man, one sick person, one dead man after having been protected from such experiences for years in his father's palace. But he immediately grasps these three chance occurrences as signs for an essential condition of the world. Descartes tried to grasp the essence or essential structure of bodies, by examining a piece of wax—which is quite different from the chemist who analyzes the ingredients of a certain substance. The whole field of mathematics provides impressive evidence for essences of this kind. The animal has a vague conception of plurality which is completely attached to things perceived in their shapes and arrangements. Man alone is able to separate the concept or class of "threeness," as a "collection" of three things from these things

49

themselves, and to operate with the "number" 3 as an independent object according to formal rules for producing a series of such objects. Yet, what mathematics discovers about the relations of nonsensible entities in an axiomatic system is, strange to say, capable of being applied, if not today, then tomorrow with great precision to the world of real things. These are the achievements of the spirit, not of a practical, inferential intelligence. The animal cannot do anything like this.

Ideation, therefore, means to grasp the essential modes and formal structures of the world through a single case only, independent of the number of observations and inductive inferences which belong to intelligence. The knowledge so gained is then universally valid for all possible cases of the same essential nature, and for all possible subjects who think about the same case, quite independent of the accidents of the senses and the manner and degree of their stimulation. Insights so gained, therefore, are valid beyond the limits of sensory experience. They are valid not only for this world, but for all possible worlds. In technical language, we call them a priori.

This knowledge of essences fulfills two different functions. On the one hand, it provides the presuppositions, or fundamental axioms, for the positive sciences whose field of research is strictly delimited by methods of proof through observation and measurement. There are different groups of such axioms in different areas within the general system of logic, and they give direction to fruitful observation and inferences, both inductive and deductive. For metaphysics, on the other hand, whose goal is the knowledge of absolute being, the essences are, as Hegel said appropriately, "windows into the absolute." For each genuine essence which reason discovers in the world cannot be reduced to causes of a finite kind, nor can the existence of "something" characterized by such an essence be so reduced. It can only be ascribed *qua* essence to a superindividual spirit as an attribute of the superindividual being in itself (*ens a se*). And the existence of such an essence can only be understood as a secondary attribute inherent in the nature of the eternal vital impulse.

The capacity to distinguish between essence and existence is a basic characteristic of the human spirit. Not that man's capability of knowledge in general is his essential characteristic, as Leibniz observed, but that he is capable of a priori knowledge. This does not mean that there is a constant, permanent structure of reason, as Kant believed. On the contrary, this structure is always subject to historical change. What is constant is reason as a diposition and capacity to create and to shape, through the actualization of new essential insights, new forms of thought, intuition, love and value. (These forms first take shape in the minds of the leading pioneers and then are shared by the rest of mankind through participation.)

If we wish to probe more deeply into the nature of man, we must try to deal with the structure of processes which lead to the act of ideation. Whether consciously or unconsciously, man employs a technique which may be described as a tentative experimental suspension of reality. In this experimental technique the essence is peeled off, as it were, from the concrete sensory object. The animal, as we saw, still lives entirely within the domain of concrete reality. The notion of reality involves, partly, a place in space and time, a here and now and, partly, an adventitious quality as it is disclosed through sense perception from a particular perspective.

To be human means to oppose this reality with an emphatic "No." Buddha knew this when he said that it is wonderful to look upon the things of this world and terrible to be them, and when he developed his technique of de-actualizing the world and the self. Plato knew this when he envisaged the intuition of forms as a turning away of the soul from the sensory world, and the return of the soul to itself, in order to go back to the original nature and source of things. And Husserl meant the same thing when he based the intuition of essences upon a phenomenological reduction, a "canceling" or "bracketing" of the accidental coefficients of things in the world in order to bring out their essences. While I do not go along with Husserl's theory of reduction in its details, I do believe that it refers to the essential act by which the human spirit must be defined.

If we wish to know how this act of reduction takes place, we must first ask what our experience of reality is. There is no specific sensory experience that conveys the impression of reality, nor do the senses in general do so, or memory or thought. They can convey some quality (*Sosein*) of things, not their existence (*Dasein*). Existence, or a sense of reality, is derived from the experience of resistance in a world already present as given, and this experience of resistance is inherent in the vital drive, in the central life impulse of our being.[8] The reality of the external world (which is present even in dreams) is not a matter of inference, is not a perceptual experience, is not associated with an experience of objects (which occurs even in fantasy) or with a fixed position in space, arresting our attention. Reality is always a sense of resistance experienced on the lowest and most primitive stage of psychic life, or in the very center of our vital drives constantly active even in sleep and in a state of unconsciousness. In the strict organization of the characteristics of a physical thing, including color, shape and extension—an organization which we can study in pathological deficiencies of perception —there is nothing more immediate than the sense of reality. Suppose we let all colors and sensory qualities, all forms and relations of a physical thing dissolve in our consciousness, what remains naked, as it were, and without qualitative characteristics, is the powerful impression of reality itself, the impression of the reality of the world.

This original experience of reality as an experience of resistance precedes any consciousness, conception and perception. Even the strongest sensory experience is never a function of the stimulus and the normal processes of the nervous system only. A drive-attitude, whether attraction or repulsion, must also be present if there is to be even the simplest perception. A drive-attitude is an indispensable accessory condition for all possible perceptions. This explains why the resistances which the centers and fields of forces behind the physical images in the environment exercise upon the vital impulse—the images themselves are ineffective—can be experienced at a point in the temporal process of an incipient perception when it has not yet become a conscious image. Experience of reality, therefore, does not come after, but before any representation of the world.

What, then, is meant by this radical "No" of which I just spoke? What does it mean to "de-actualize" the world or to "ideate" it? It does not mean, as Husserl believed, to suspend the existential judgment which is inherent in every natural act of perception. The judgment "A is real" presupposes, as far as the predicate is concerned, the content of experience, if "real" is not to be an empty word. No, what it means is to suspend, at least tentatively, the experience of reality itself, or to annihilate the entire, indivisible, powerful impression of reality together with its affective corollates. What it means is to remove the "anguish of earthly existence" which, as Schiller wrote, is overcome only "in those regions where the pure forms dwell." For all reality, because it is reality, and regardless of what it is, is a kind of inhibiting, constraining pressure for every living being. Its corollate is "pure" anxiety, an anxiety without an object. If reality means resistance, the canceling of reality can only be the kind of ascetic act by which we suspend the operation of the vital impulse in relation to which the world appears as resistance, and which is the precondition for all sensory experience and its accidental qualities. Drives and senses belong together. This is the reason why Plato said that philosophy is a process of "dying" (to the body), and this is the reason why every type of extreme rationalism is ultimately founded upon an "ascetic ideal."

This act of de-actualization, or de-realizing the world, can be performed only by a being which we have called "spirit." Only spirit in its form as pure will can, by an act of will—an act of inhibition—put out of action that center of vital impulses which we recognized as the key to reality.

Man is the kind of being who, by means of the spirit, can take an ascetic attitude toward life. He can suppress and repress his own vital drives and deny them the nourishment of perceptual images and representations. Compared with the animal that always says "Yes," to reality, even when it avoids it and flees from it, man is the being who can say "No," the "ascetic of life," the protestant par excellence, against mere reality. This has nothing to do with any question of value or *Weltanschauung*. It does not matter whether we follow Buddha and say that this ascent of the spirit into the unreal sphere of essence is the ultimate goal and good of man because reality is inherently evil (*omne ens est malum*) or whether, as I believe, we must try to return from the sphere of essences to the reality of the world in order to improve it (in this case existence is, to begin with, neutral with respect to good and evil) and whether we envisage the true life and destiny of man in terms of an eternal rhythmic movement between idea and reality, spirit and instinct—and in the reconciliation of this constant tension.

At any rate, as compared with the animal whose existence is, as it were, Philistinism incarnate, man is the eternal Faust, the creature always seeking and desiring (*bestia cupidissima rerum novarum*), never at peace with his environment, always anxious to break through the barriers of his life here and now, always striving to transcend his environment, including his own state of being. For Freud, too, man is the being who represses his instincts.[4]

Only because man has this capacity for repression, not now and then, but as a permanent capacity, does he accomplish two things. First, he erects a superstructure of ideas above the world of sensory experience. Secondly, by this very means, he makes accessible to his spirit the latent energy of the repressed drives. In other words, man is capable of sublimating his instinctual energy into spiritual activity.

III *spirit and life*

Another crucial question arises at this point: Is spirit the product of asceticism, repression and sublimation, or does spirit merely receive its energy by these means? Is the technique of repression—which, in turn, is conditioned by the inhibiting act of the will—simply a means for manifesting the spirit in man, or is the spirit itself, in its very nature, principles and laws, a product of repression and sublimation? In my opinion, the negative acts, the "No," thrown against reality, the cancellation and repression of drives, do not determine the being of spirit. They only determine the supply of energy available to the spirit and thus its power to manifest itself in the word. The spirit is, as we said, ultimately an attribute of Being itself which becomes manifest in man, in the unity of self-concentration characteristic of the person. But in its pure form spirit is originally without power, energy or activity. In order to gain the smallest degree of energy and activity, asceticism, the repression and sublimation of instincts must be added to the pure form of the spirit.

From this perspective, we gain an insight into two conceptions of the spirit which have played an important role in the history of the idea of man. The first theory, developed by the Greeks, attributes to spirit not only a unique nature and autonomy, but also energy and activity—yes, the highest degree of power. This is the classical theory of man. It is part of a total world view according to which the permanent nature of the universe, remaining unchanged throughout its historical development, is so constructed that the higher forms of being from the Godhead to brute matter are also the more powerful ones, the causal agents and creative modes of being. The apex of such a world then is a spiritual and omnipotent God, a God who is omnipotent because he is spirit.

The second theory—which we may call the negative theory—takes the opposite point of view: spirit (if this be an admissible term) or, at least all culture-producing activities of man, including all logical, moral, aesthetic and creative acts, are possible only as a result of man's capacity to repress his impulses.

I reject both theories. Instead, I claim that spirit has its own nature and autonomy, but lacks an original energy of its own. The negative acts of inhibition, which originate in the spiritual act of willing, provide energy for the spirit which, to begin with, is impotent and consists only of a group of pure "intentions." They do not produce the spirit itself.

Here are some examples for the negative theory of man: Buddha's doctrine of salvation, Schopenhauer's doctrine of the self-negation of the will to live, the remarkable book by Paul Alsberg, *The Riddle of Mankind,* and, finally the theories of Freud, especially in *Beyond the Pleasure Principle.* According to Buddha, who understood with profound insight that the sense of reality involves suffering caused by the experience of resistance, the meaning of human existence is the extinction of man as a subject of desire, or the passage into a purely contemplative world of essences—into nothingness or Nirvana in the language of myth. Buddha does not have a positive theory of the spirit, neither with regard to man nor with regard to the Ground of Being. He has a technique, a "sacred path of knowledge" by which suffering is overcome. He knows the causal order of things in which, by means of this technique of canceling reality through suspension of desire—"thirst," as he called it, the sensory world and the physical and mental processes disappear and fall away piece by piece, along with the sensory qualities, shapes, relations and forms of space and time.

Schopenhauer sees the characteristic difference between animal and man in the animal's inability to perform the redeeming negation of the will to live which man, in his highest types, is capable of achieving. It is this negation which for Schopenhauer is the source of all higher forms of consciousness and knowledge in metaphysics, art and in the ethics of sympathy. Alsberg, a disciple of Schopenhauer's, is quite correct in pointing out that the general conviction of our cultural world—that there is an essential difference between man and animal—cannot be justified on morphological, physiological or psychological grounds. He has expanded Schopenhauer's doctrine by asserting that "the principle of humanity" consists exclusively in man's being capable of releasing his organs from the struggle for survival as an individual or as a species in favor of developing tools, language and concepts. The latter are explained in terms of the principle of canceling sensory organs and functions or in terms of Mach's principle of achieving the highest possible "economy" with respect to sensory contents. Alsberg refuses explicitly to define man in terms of spirit and reason. Reason, which he identifies erroneously—as did his teacher Schopenhauer—with discursive thought, especially with the formation of concepts, is for him the consequence of language, not its source. Language itself is conceived as a nonmaterial tool whose purpose is to eliminate the work of the sensory organs. The cause for the origin of this "principle of humanity," this tendency of life to eliminate its organs and to put tools and symbols in place of organic functions—thus, the cause also for the growth of the human brain in a morphological and physiological sense—is, according to Alsberg, the particular defective organic adaptation of man to his environment: his lack, in other words, of those specific organic adaptations (grasping and climbing feet, claws, canine teeth and hairy fur) that are found among the primates, man's closest relatives. Thus, what is called "spirit" is for Alsberg nothing but a late surrogate for defective organic adaptation. In the language of Alfred Adler (who explains special human talents in this way), it is a kind of overcompensation for the constitutional organic inferiority of the species man.

The theories of Freud also fall into this category. The term "repression of instincts and affects" was already used by Schopenhauer in order to explain certain "delusional ideas," as he called them. It is generally known how brilliantly Freud developed these ideas for an understanding of the origin of neuroses. But, according to Freud, the same repressions which are supposed to explain the nature of neuroses are also supposed to produce, provided the repressed energy of the instincts is sublimated, nothing less than the capacity for every kind of higher cultural development, or as Freud says explicitly, the specificity of the human constitution itself. Thus we read: "The development of man, it seems to me, does not require a different explanation from the development of animals. What may be observed in the minority of individuals as a restless striving toward perfection can be understood quite naturally as the consequence of the displacement of drives on which the most valuable achievements of human culture are based." It has not been sufficiently noted that Freud, with his dualistic theory of libido and death instinct, shows a strange (often conscious) affinity not only with Schopenhauer but with Buddha. According to both, all modes of existence, from the material world on up through plant, animal and man to the "sacred knowledge" of the saint, are, as it were, forms of an arrested procession into quiet nothingness and eternal death. Freud ascribes (mistakenly, I believe) to the organism as such a tendency toward equilibrium and protection against stimulation. Even the motor system in animals, which is added to the nutritive, growth and reproductive systems in plants and interposed between animal and environment, is interpreted as a reflection of the basically sadistic and destructive death instinct, or of the primitive longing of all life to return to an inorganic state.[1]

I do not accept any of the theses of these negative theories. They are all one-sided formulations with respect to vital values only. I believe, for example, that the culture of India did not even know the specifically Greek and occidental category of spirit. All Indian systems are forms of biologism, whether positive or negative, and this with respect to the uniqueness of inorganic life as well as to the uniqueness of spirit. But these are minor matters.

The crucial weakness of every kind of negative theory is that it has no answer to the basic questions: What is it that negates in man? What is it that denies the will to live?

What is it that represses instincts? Why does the repressed energy in one case lead to neurosis, whereas in another case it is sublimated into culturally creative activity? What is the goal of sublimation? Why do the principles of spirit coincide, at least partially, with the principles of being? Finally, what is the purpose of repression, sublimation and negation of the will to live—for the sake of what goals and values? Alsberg, too, must answer the questions: What is it that produces the atrophy of organic functions? What is it that invents tools both material and symbolic? Are organs really discarded, and this only for the sake of the values and goals characteristic of animals, for the sake of survival? The concept of "need" will not do as an explanation. (It was already vastly overrated by Lamarck to explain the formation of organs.) And why did this badly adjusted species called man not die out as hundreds of other species did? How is it possible that this being practically condemned to death, this sick, retarded, suffering animal, with its basic attitude of anxiously covering and protecting its badly adapted and overly vulnerable organs, could save itself through the "principle of humanity," through civilization and culture or through the principle of objective progress and growth of the forms of spirit? How did it escape from this "dead end" which I grant on biological grounds? Surely not through reason or spirit, which are supposed to have come into existence only as a result of asceticism, repression and discarding of organs. It has been said that man has a surplus of instinctual energy as part of his constitution and that this is the cause of repression; but it is likely to be the other way around. Surplus of energy is the effect of repression, not its cause.

The negative theory invariably presupposes what it is

supposed to explain: namely, spirit, reason, the autonomy of the spirit, and its identity with the principles of being. It is precisely the spirit that initiates the repression of instincts. It does so in the following manner: Subject to its own ideas and values, the spiritual "will" withdraws from the opposing vital impulses the images necessary for action. At the same time, it lures the drives with a bait of appropriate images in order to coordinate the vital impulses so that they will execute the project set by the spirit. The process that consists in the inhibition and release of vital impulses through the spiritual will I call "direction" (*Lenkung*). The process of presenting ideas and values, which are then realized through the impulses, I call "guidance" (*Leitung*).

There is one thing the spirit cannot do: it cannot generate or cancel the instinctual energy; it cannot enlarge or diminish it. It can only call upon energy complexes which will then act through the organism in order to accomplish what the spirit "wills." But there is something positive, not just in regulating the drives, but also in the goal achieved thereby. It is a process of gaining power and activity for the spirit, inner freedom and autonomy. In short, it is a process of making the spirit come to life. This alone deserves to be called sublimation, not a mystical transaction by which spirit is generated from repression and by which new spiritual qualities are supposed to be created.

Thus we come back to the classical theory of spirit. It is, as I said, just as false as the negative theory, but since it has prevailed almost throughout the whole history of western philosophy, its error is more dangerous. This classical theory originates in the Greek conception of the mind. It is the doctrine of the autonomous power of the idea, or the view that the (rational) idea has an original power, activity and energy. First conceived by the Greeks, this view has become a basic conception of a large segment of bourgeois thought in the western world.[2] Whether this classical theory states, as in Plato and Aristotle, that the ideas or forms are the creative powers which transform nonbeing ($\mu\grave{\eta}\ \delta\gamma$) or the potentialities inherent in prime matter into the objects of this world; whether the theory appears in the theistic version of the Judaeo-Christian tradition, according to which God is nothing but pure spirit, responsible for guidance and direction and endowed with a positive, creative, yes, all-powerful will; whether this theory appears in pantheistic form, as in Fichte, or in the panlogical system of Hegel *—in all these various manifestations the classical theory suffers from the same fallacy: spirit and idea are envisaged as endowed with original, creative power. Spirit is said to be the powerful, all-powerful principle even without the vital impulse.

Here the great opponents of the classical theory, the physical or biological naturalists such as Epicurus, Hobbes, Machiavelli, La Mettrie, Schopenhauer, Marx and Freud score a critical point. However, in their legitimate opposition to the classical theory, they also give up the truth contained in this theory: the truth that spirit is autonomous in its being and laws. Thus, they invalidate with their criticism any autonomous theorizing, including their own naturalistic theories. For the autonomy of spirit is the basic presupposition for the idea of truth and the possibility of discovering the truth.

* In Hegel world history is the self-unfolding of the Divine Idea according to the dialectical law and man is nothing but the growing self-consciousness, the consciousness of freedom, which the eternal, spiritual Deity realizes in man and history. [In the original this passage occurs in the text. Trans.]

The classical theory appears in two main versions: first, in the doctrine of the spiritual substance of man; secondly, in the doctrine according to which there is only a single spirit in relation to which all the other spirits are but modes of subsidiary centers of activity (Cf. Averroes, Spinoza, Kant, Fichte, Hegel, Schelling, Von Hartmann). The doctrine of the soul as a substance rests on the unjustifiable application of the "thing" category to the soul—in its older versions, on the application of the categories of "matter" and "form" to the relationship of body and soul (St. Thomas Aquinas).

Both attempts to apply objective or cosmological categories to the essential nature of man miss their mark. The spiritual center of activity, which we have called the person in man, is not a substance but a hierarchical structure of acts, in which one of them assumes direction and guidance in accordance with the goal of a value or idea with which the individual happens to "identify himself." But let us not pursue this criticism in detail. The basic fallacy common to all classical theories is deeply rooted in its world view as a whole. It is a fallacy to assume that the world in which we live is so ordered that, with the superior meaning and value revealed in higher forms of being, there goes a corresponding increase in power and energy.

Thus, in our view, one error is as great as the other. It is a mistake to assume that the higher forms of being—for example, life as compared with the inorganic world, or consciousness with unconscious life, or spirit as compared with the lower forms of consciousness in man or the outside world —develop genetically from the lower forms of being. This is the mistake of materialism and naturalism. It is also a mistake to assume that the higher modes of being are the *causes* of the lower, or that there is something like a life-power, an active consciousness, with an inherently powerful and creative spirit. This is the mistake of vitalism and idealism. The negative theory leads to the false view of a universal mechanism, the classical theory to the untenable doctrine of a so-called teleological world view which is behind the entire theology of the Western world. The same idea, which I previously put forth in my *Ethics*, was recently expressed by Nicolai Hartmann in the succinct formulation: "The higher categories of being of value are inherently the weaker ones."

The movement of forces and energies which determines human existence and the contingencies of nature in our world do not run from the higher to the lower, but from the lower to the higher. The inorganic world in its autonomy displays a proud independence. Plant and animal face man in proud independence; the animal is more dependent upon the existence of plant life than vice versa. For, the direction of life toward the animal represents not only a gain, but also a loss as compared with the plant life, since the animal is deprived of the direct contact with the inorganic world which the plant has through its mode of nourishment. Again, the masses of mankind in history display a similar independence in the autonomy and inertia of their movements, as compared with the higher forms of human existence.

From our human perspective, it almost looks like an accident of good fortune or grace when we think that the earth or some distant star has become a bearer of life, or when we see that the autonomous movements of masses move in the direction of tolerating a genius in their midst, not to speak of accepting his ideas and values for their own interests and passions. How rare an accident when the ethically good person succeeds in the world or achieves what we call "historical greatness" and power in history. Brief and rare are the periods of cultural flowering in human history. Brief and rare is beauty in its tenderness and vulnerability.

Spirit is originally devoid of power and efficacy, and the more this is so, the purer it is. The original order of relations holding between the higher and lower forms of being and categories of value, on the one hand, and the forces and energies in which these forms are realized, on the other, may be expressed as follows: "To begin with, the lowest forms are the most powerful, and the highest the most impotent." Every higher form of being is relatively impotent with respect to the lower: it is realized, not through its own power, but through the energy of the lower forms. The process of life has it own structure unfolding in time, but it is realized exclusively through the material substance and energy of the inorganic world.

Spirit and life are related in the same way. It is true that spirit can *acquire* energy through the process of sublimation. It is true that the vital impulses can enter into the autonomous and meaningful structure of the spirit and, in so doing, lend power to the spirit in the individual and in history. But, to begin with and inherently, the spirit has no energy of its own. The higher forms of being may determine the essence or the essential regions of the world, but these essences are realized only through another principle that belongs to Ground of Being as intimately as the spiritual principle. This is the principle which we have called vital impulse, or the image-producing "vital fantasy" out of which a sense of reality emerges.

The most powerful forces are the centers of energy in the

inorganic world which represent the most primitive manifestations of this vital impulse. They are "blind," as it were, to any idea, form or meaning. According to contemporary physics, it is likely that these centers are not even subject to a strict causal order in their interaction, but only to the accidental order of statistical regularity. Only man as a living being introduces law and order into nature, not from a rational, but from a biological necessity (that is, in order to be able to act) by virtue of the fact that the sensory organs or functions indicate more the regular than the irregular processes in the world. Later, reason interprets this regularity as a natural law.

It is not lawfulness in the ontological sense which is behind the chaos of chance and caprice, but it is chaos which is to be found behind the laws in the formal mechanical sense. If this view that all natural laws are ultimately statistical laws only, that all natural processes (including those on a submicroscopic level) are total processes resulting from the interaction of energy centers governed by chance—if this view should prevail, it would mean a complete transformation of our conception of nature. The true natural laws would then be so-called structural laws (*Gestaltgesetze*), laws which prescribe a certain temporal rhythm in natural processes and, following from these, certain static structures of physical objects.[8] Now, since within the sphere of life, in its physiological and psychic aspects, only laws of a structural kind are valid, although not necessarily the material laws of physics only, this new view would again make possible a unified conception of lawfulness in nature.

From this point of view it might be possible to extend the concept of sublimation to all natural processes. Sublimation would then designate the natural process by which energies of a lower sphere of being, in the course of evolution, are made available to higher forms of being and becoming. For example, the energy exchange among electrons would give rise to the structure of the atom, or, the energies in the inorganic world would be pressed into service on behalf of life. The evolution of man would then represent the last act of sublimation in nature, at least until now. It manifests itself in two ways: in the channeling of more and more external energy absorbed by the organism into the most complicated processes we know (the stimulation of the cerebral cortex) and, at the same time, in the analogous psychic process of sublimation as the transformation of instinctual energy into spiritual activity.

We encounter the same relationship of spirit and life in the field of history. Hegel's thesis that history is an unfolding of mere ideas is surely untenable. On the contrary, Marx was right: ideas which do not have interests and passions behind them, that is, energies derived from the vital and instinctual sphere of man, invariably tend to make fools of themselves in history. Nonetheless, history does show, on the whole and in general, an increasing scope in the power of reason. But this is the case only by virtue of the fact that ideas and values tend to become appropriated by the great instinctual tendencies in social groups and by the common interests that link them. Here, too, we must be much more modest in our view of the influence of the human spirit and will upon the course of history.

Spirit and will never mean anything else but guidance and direction. And this means that the spirit as such presents ideas to the drives and that the will supplies to, or withdraws from, the drives (which must always be present first) such images and representations as may lead to the complete realization of these ideas. The central spiritual will, therefore, originally has no guiding power over the drives themselves, but only over the modification of their (psychic) representations. A direct struggle of the pure will against the instinct is impossible—a struggle without the representation of ideas or without interference of ideas that are presented or withheld. Whenever the struggle is put in such direct terms, it only strengthens the tendency of the drives to go in their own direction. That was the experience of St. Paul when he said that the law was running around like a roaring lion in order to attack men with sin. In more recent times, William James has made some profound observations on this point. The will always achieves the opposite of what it intends when, instead of aiming at a higher value, the realization of which attracts the impulse and makes us forget what is "bad," it is directed merely toward inhibiting and at struggling against the impulse whose goal is condemned as "bad" by our conscience. Thus, man must learn to live with himself and to tolerate even those inclinations which he recognizes as bad and perverse. He must not fight them directly, but he must learn to overcome them indirectly by investing his energies in worthwhile tasks which are accessible to him and which his conscience recognizes as good and decent. There is, as Spinoza saw with great insight, a deep truth in the doctrine of the "nonresistance" to evil.

The process of becoming human represents the highest sublimation known to us and, at the same time, the most intimate fusion of all the essential stages of nature. For man unifies within himself all the essential stages of existence, especially of life—at least in their *essential* aspects, not in their accidental variations and still less in their quantitative distribution. The world view sketched here cuts through the dualism that has prevailed for so many centuries: the dualism between a teleological and a mechanistic explanation of reality.[4]

This train of thought, obviously, cannot stop short of the highest form of Being—the world-ground. Even the Being which is its own cause (*causa sui*) and upon which everything else depends cannot, in so far as the attribute of spirit applies to it, possess any original power of energy. Instead, it is the other attribute—the *natura naturans* in the highest Being, the all-powerful drive charged with infinite images—which must account for reality and for the contingent qualities of this reality which are never determined unequivocably by the essential laws and ideas. If we call the spiritual attributes of the highest Ground of Being *deitas,* then we cannot impute any positive, creative power to what we call spirit or Godhead in this highest ground. Thus, the idea of a creation *ex nihilo* is untenable. If there is in the highest Ground of Being this tension between spirit and drive, then the relationship of this Being to the world must be different.

We put this relationship as follows: In order to realize its *deitas,* or its inherent plenitude of ideas and values, the Ground of Being was compelled to release the world-creative drive. It was compelled, as it were, to pay the price of this world process in order to realize its own essence in and through this temporal process. And this Being would deserve to be called divine being only to the degree to which it realizes its eternal *deitas* in the processes of world history and in or through man. In fact, this process, essentially timeless, but manifesting itself in time for our finite experience, can approach its goal—the self-realization of the Godhead—only to the degree to which what we call "world" becomes the perfect body of the eternal substance.

An assimilation of the forms of being and value with the actual, effective energies can take place only in the raging tempest of the world. Yes, in the course of this development there may even occur a gradual reversal in the original relationship, according to which the higher forms of being are the weaker, the lower forms the stronger. To put it differently: Spirit, originally impotent, and the demonic drive originally blind to all spiritual ideas and values, may fuse in the growing process of ideation, or spiritualization, in the sublimation of the drives and in the simultaneous actualization, or vitalization, of the spirit. This interaction and exchange represent the goal of finite being and becoming. Theism erroneously puts this goal at the beginning.

We have climbed rather high. Let us return to the problem of human nature which is closer to our experience.

In modern times, the classical theory found its most effective exponent in Descartes. We are only now in the process of discarding it. By dividing all substances into two, a thinking substance (mind) and an extended substance (matter), and by arguing that man alone consisted of the mutual interaction of these two substances, Descartes is responsible for a host of the most serious fallacies about human nature. For this division he paid the nonsensical price of depriving both plants and animals of psychic life and of explaining the "appearance" of such psychic life in animals and plants (which had always been taken for granted) as the result of an anthropomorphic "empathy" on our part with the processes in the organic world. Conversely, he explained everything that was not human consciousness and thought according to strictly mechanistic principles. The result was a fantastic exaggeration of the unique position of man now completely torn loose from the maternal arms of nature. In fact, the category of life itself and its phenomena was thrown out of the world with one stroke of the pen. For Descartes, the world consists only of thinking "points" and of a gigantic mechanism to be explored mathematically. There is only one thing of value in this theory: the new autonomy and sovereignty accorded to the spirit.*

That there is no such a thing as a substantial soul located, as Descartes believed, in the pineal gland is perfectly obvious because there is no central point, neither in the brain nor elsewhere in the body, where all sensitive nerve filaments run together, or where all nerve processes meet. It is also false to assume, as Descartes did, that psychic life consists of nothing but consciousness and is exclusively bound up with the cerebral cortex. Psychiatric research has shown that the psychic functions chiefly responsible for man's character, especially those that belong to affects and drives (these, as we have seen, are the basic forms of psychic life) do not have a corresponding physiological process in the cortex or cere-

* In Descartes, however, spirit is interpreted as reason; and reason, in turn, mixed up with the intellect. Yet Descartes recognized that spirit was superior to the organic, living world. In the medieval doctrine which identified spiritual soul with the forma corporeitatis, spirit did not have this superior status. [In the original this passage occurs in the text. Trans.]

72

brum, but in the region of the cerebellum, partly in the central gray opening of the third ventricle, partly in the thalamus which mediates, as a central switchboard, between sensory and affective stimuli. Moreover, the system of ductless glands (thyroid, gonads, pituitary, hypophysis, adrenal)— whose functions determine the affective, instinctual life along with human growth in height and size, giant-growth and dwarf-growth, probably even racial characteristics—has turned out to be the real mediating agency between the organism as a whole, including its structural development, on the one hand, and the small accessory part of psychic life which we call waking consciousness. It is the entire body, and not only the brain, which has become the physiological field corresponding to psychic processes. Nobody today would take seriously the kind of superficial connection between a mental substance and a physical substance as Descartes envisaged it.

Philosophers, medical men and natural scientists concerned with the mind-body problem converge more and more toward a unified conception. It is one and the same life which, in its inwardness, has a psychic structure and which, in its being for others, has a physical structure. This is not refuted by the argument that the "self" or "ego" is a simple unitary entity, whereas the body is a complex society of cells. Contemporary physiology has completely discarded the conception of a society of cells, just as it has broken with the conception that the functions of the nervous system operate according to a merely additive (that is, non-holistic) pattern and are determined both locally and morphologically at their point of origin. Of course, if we say with Descartes that the physical organism is nothing but a machine, and a machine in a strict sense of the mechanistic conception of nature now completely discarded in theoretical physics and chemistry, or if we overlook, as Descartes did, that the affective and instinctive life is independent of and prior to, the world of consciousness, or if we identify all psychic life with conscious life and overlook the vast fields of psychic functions split off from the conscious ego, and finally, if we deny the repression of affects and overlook the phenomena of amnesia possible for whole phases of life, then, indeed, we may come to postulate a false dualism: psychic unity and simplicity, on the one side, and infinite multiplicity of a physical substance, on the other. This model of the soul is just as false in its exaggerated centralization as the older model of physiological processes based on an exaggerated mechanism.

In sharp contrast to all these theories we may say: The physiological and psychic processes of life are strictly identical in an ontological sense. They differ only as phenomena. But even as phenomena they are strictly identical in their structural laws and in the rhythm of their processes. Both processes are nonmechanical, the physiological as well as the psychic. Both are oriented toward a goal and toward wholeness (teleoclitic and holistic). The physiological processes are all the more the lower (not the higher), as are the segments of the nervous system in which they take place. The psychic processes are also more unified and goal-directed the more primitive they are. Both processes are but two aspects of the process of life, which is one and nonmechanical in its structure and in the interaction of its functions.

Thus, what we call "physiological" and "psychological" are but two ways of looking at one and the same process of life. There is a biology "from within" and a biology

74

"from without." The biology from without moves from the formal structure of the organism to the real living processes, but it must never forget that every living form, from the ultimate constituents of the cell to the cells, tissues, organs and the organism itself, is dynamically carried forward and newly formed through the process of life. It is the "formative functions" of the organs, in contradistinction to the operational functions, which produce the static (and anatomical) forms of the organic material with the cooperation of the physical-chemical "situation." This conception has gained ground in all the sciences concerned with this famous problem. The old "psychomechanical" parallelism of body and soul is today just as outmoded as the "interaction theory" which Lotze revived, or the scholastic doctrine of the soul as the *forma corporeitatis.*

The gap which Descartes opened up with his dualism of extension and consciousness as essential attributes of body and soul is now being closed almost to a point where we can grasp the unity of life. When a dog sees a piece of meat and gastric juices begin to flow—this is for Descartes an absolute miracle. Why? Because he had thrown the instinctive and affective life out of the soul and, at the same time, had asked for a purely chemical-physical explanation of living processes, even with respect to their structural laws. On the psychic side, he had excluded the vital drive of the appetite which is as much a condition for the optic event of perceiving food as the external stimulus. The latter, incidentally, is never, as Descartes believed, the condition of the perceptual content, but only for the *present* perception of this content here and now, which as part of the body-image is quite independent of consciousness. Conversely, on the physiological side, he did not consider the flow of gastric juices, which corresponds to the appetite, as a genuine living process rooted in the physiological unity of functions and its structure. Instead, he envisaged it as a process which takes its course quite independently of the central nervous system according to strictly chemical reactions occurring in the stomach as soon as food is present. What would Descartes have said if confronted with the results of Heyder's work, according to which the mere suggestion of eating food can have the same effect as the actual eating?

The fallacy, Descartes' basic fallacy, is evident: the system of drives in men and animals is completely disregarded—his treatise on the "passions" to the contrary notwithstanding. But it is precisely this system that constitutes the essential unity and that mediates between every genuine living process and the contents of consciousness. Descartes and other older physiologists thought that functional unity in the physiological sense was a localizable process of immediate causal action in a mechanical system proceeding from rigid, morphologically determined points in the organism and completely subject to mechanical principles. But that is not the case. The physiological "function" is fundamentally an independent (autonomous) rhythmic structure, a dynamic temporal structure, by no means rigidly fixed at a specific locality, but with a capacity for singling out, yes, even creating its own functional field within the existing cellular substratum. An additive organic reaction of a definite and rigid sort does not even take place among those physiological functions for which there is no conscious correlate, not even in the case of so simple a reflex as the patella reflex. The organism, even within a physiological context, can achieve the same end by employing the physical structure and substratum in rather different ways. Phenomenologically speaking, the physiological processes of the organism are just as "meaningful" as the conscious processes, and the latter just as "stupid" (blind) as the organic processes. For example, if, in the regenerative process of a wounded organism, two heads appear instead of one, this is analogous to the psychic complex of a blind repetition compulsion, the need to restore the same whole complex or scene, as in the case of the individual who always feels he is "deceived" or is a "victim" regardless of the circumstances.

In my opinion, contemporary research should be engaged in a methodological inquiry to test, on the largest possible scale, how the *same* modes of organic behavior are caused and changed, on the one hand, by external stimuli of a physical-chemical nature, and, on the other, by psychic stimuli—suggestion, hypnosis, all forms of psychotherapy and changes in the social environment, which produce more illness than we think. Thus we should guard against over-emphasizing purely physiological explanations. According to our present knowledge, a gastric ulcer may be caused as much by psychological factors as by chemical-physical processes. Not only nervous diseases, but organic illnesses as well have definite psychic correlates. We can weigh both kinds of influence—the influence through the channel of conscious stimulation and the influence through the channel of external stimulation upon the same life process—in quantitative terms so that we can economize with regard to one and make more use of the other. Sexual excitation may be induced by physical means as much as by lascivious pictures and books. Even the basic process of life called "death" may be caused through a sudden emotional shock as much as through a bullet from a pistol.

All these phenomena are but different modes by which we gain access, in experience and through efforts of control, to the same ontologically unified process of life. Even the highest mental functions—relational thinking—have physiological parallels. Finally, according to this view, we must also say that the spiritual acts which draw their energy from the living sphere of drives and do not manifest themselves in our experience without this energy, these spiritual acts, too, always have a physiological and a psychic aspect running parallel with each other. The fact that, in the Western world, the sciences concerned with man, the natural sciences and medicine, have occupied themselves primarily with the human body and have tried to influence living processes, especially through external means, is another manifestation of the extremely one-sided interest characteristic of Western technology. If living processes appear to us much more accessible from without than through the channel of consciousness, this need not say anything about the true relationship of psyche and body, but may only reflect a one-sided interest cultivated over centuries. Medicine in India, for example, shows an opposite orientation—just as one-sided—toward the psychic side of life.

Psychophysical life is one. This unity is a fact for all forms of life, including man. There is not the slightest reason to think that there is more than a difference in degree between the psychic life in man and in the animal, or to ascribe to this body-soul the special kind of origin or future that we find in the theistic doctrine of creation or in the traditional doctrine of immortality. The Mendelian laws are just as valid for the structure of the psychic character as for any physical characteristics. There are, to be sure, considerable differences between man and animal with respect to their psychic functions, but the physiological differences are just as considerable and even more so than the morphological differences. As compared with the animal, man employs a disproportionately large part of the materials he assimilates to create nervous substance, but the use of this material is surprisingly small as far as the formation of anatomically observable entities is concerned. In comparison with the animal, a very large part of this material is transformed into purely functional brain energy.

This process is the physiological correlate of the same process which, in psychological language, we call repression and sublimation. Whereas the human organism in its sensory and motor functions is not essentially superior to the animal, the distribution of energy between the cerebrum and all other organic systems is completely different. The human brain enjoys a much greater supply of nourishment (energy) than the brain of the animal, since it displays the most intensive and manifold gradients of energy, and since its excitations run a course which is much less rigidly localized. Where we find a general inhibition of assimilation, the brain is affected last and, as compared with other organs, to the least degree. The cerebral cortex preserves and concentrates the entire life history of the organism and its prehistory. Since every process of excitation in the brain invariably transforms the entire structure, the "same" physiological process can never be repeated—a fact which corresponds exactly to the basic law of psychic causality according to which a given psychological phenomenon can only be explained in terms of the entire past chain of experience, and never in terms of the single event which is its temporal antecedent. Since the excitations in the cortex never cease, not even during sleep, and since the structural elements are renewed at each instant, an enormous surplus of fantasy may be expected. This surplus runs its course even without external stimulation and breaks through as soon as our waking consciousness and its censor relax. It is a completely original phenomenon, increasingly restricted by sensory perceptions but not produced by them. The psychic stream runs its course with the same continuity as the physiological chain of excitations through the rhythm of waking and sleeping.

The human brain also seems to be the actual organ of death to a much higher degree than in the animal. This is to be expected from the increased centralization and localization of all living processes in the activity of the brain. We know from a series of experiments that a dog or a horse whose cortices have been removed can still perform a great many activities which man could not perform any more under these conditions. These facts, and others of a similar kind, are fully explained by the theory that the human psyche represents a much more highly unified structure than that of the animal. There is no need to postulate a soul as a special substance.

Thus it is neither body and soul nor brain and mind that set up an essential dualism. We may say that the mind-body problem has lost the metaphysical significance it has had for centuries. Instead, the dualism which we encounter in man and which we experience ourselves is of a higher order: it is the antithesis between spirit and life.

If we envisage the "psychic" and the "physical" as two

aspects of the same life process, to which correspond two modes of observing and describing the same phenomenon, then there must be an x which makes these different observations and which must transcend the antithesis between body and soul. This x is nothing but the spirit—never, as we saw, an objective phenomenon itself, but "objectifying" everything else. If life is a nonspatial, temporal kind of being—"the organism is an event," as Jennings observed—and if all the apparently static forms of the body are carried forward and sustained by this life process, then what we call spirit is not only transspatial, but transtemporal as well. The intentions of the spirit intersect, as it were, with the temporal processes of life. The spiritual act is indirectly dependent, in so far as it requires energy, upon the temporal processes of life and is, as it were, imbedded in them.

As different as life and spirit are in their essential being, they are mutually related to each other in man. Spirit infuses life with ideas, but only life is capable of initiating and realizing the spiritual activity, from its simplest act to the achievement of a task of great spiritual content.

The relationship between spirit and life, which we have just described, has often been misunderstood by a whole group of philosophical theories about man. I shall first briefly sketch those which may be called naturalistic theories. Among these, there are two major types: (1) a one-sidedly mechanistic conception, and (2) a one-sidedly vitalistic conception.

The mechanistic theories overlook, to begin with, the uniqueness of the category of life. Thus they must misunderstand the nature of spirit. These theories appear in two traditional forms: One is derived from the ancient world, from the doctrines of Democritus, Epicurus and Lucretius Carus. This type found its most perfect expression in La Mettrie's *"l'homme machine,"* which as the title indicates is an attempt to reduce psychic phenomena, without distinguishing them from spirit, to the corresponding phenomena in the organism subject only to physical or chemical laws. The other type was developed most clearly in the British empirical tradition. Hume's *Treatise of Human Nature* is its perfect model. In recent times, Ernst Mach came closest to this conception of man when he represented the ego, or self, as a kind of nodal point in which the sense data cohere with particular density.

In both varieties, the formal mechanism is pushed to an extreme. The only difference is that, in the one case, perceptual phenomena are to be understood in terms of processes which are determined by the principles of mechanics, whereas, in the other case, the basic concepts of physical science—including the concepts of substance and causality—are derived from the sense data as the ultimate constituents of experience and from the laws of association among impressions and ideas. The fallacy of both types is to overlook the fact that life has a uniqueness and autonomy of its own.

The second type of naturalistic theory, vitalism, takes "life" as the basic category of man, including spirit, thus vastly overestimating the scope of the principle of life. The human spirit is understood as a late product of development of the instinctive life of man. Along these lines, pragmatism (Charles S. Peirce, William James, F. C. Schiller and John Dewey) has tried to derive the forms and laws of thought from the respective modes of human work and activity (*Homo faber*). Nietzsche tried to explain the forms of thought as necessary vital functions of the "will to power" inherent in life. Recently, Vaihinger developed a modified version of this theory.[5]

Surveying the different versions of the vitalistic conception of man, we may distinguish three varieties. They differ according to whether (1) the food drives, (2) the reproductive and sexual instincts, or (3) the drive for power are chosen as the original and dominant system of drives. "Man is what he eats," as Vogt put it crudely. On a much more profound level, and in the context of Hegel's philosophy of history, Karl Marx developed a similar conception according to which man does not make history, but history makes man, especially economic history or the history of the "material modes of production." According to this view, the history of spiritual achievements in art, science, philosophy and the law does not have an inner logic and continuity of its own. This continuity and autonomous causality are transferred to the progress of economic life which, according to Marx, produces at each particular stage in history a peculiar spiritual world in the form of the well-known "superstructure." [6]

The conception according to which man is primarily determined by a will to power or desire for respect originated historically with Machiavelli, Thomas Hobbes and the great theorists of the absolute state. More recently, it has been revised and expanded in Nietzsche's theory on the will to power and in a medical, psychological context, in Adler's theory of the primacy of the drive for superiority. The third group comprises those theories according to which spirit is a form of sublimated libido, its symbolic and distilled superstructure, as it were. Human culture and all its products then are the product of repressed and sublimated libido. Schopenhauer described sexual love as "the focal point of the will to life"; * and the early Freud, before he came to adopt the death instinct, pushed this conception of man to its extreme limits. [7]

All these natural theories, whether of a mechanistic or of a vitalistic type, must be rejected. The vitalistic version, to be sure, deserves credit for discovering that what is truly creative and powerful in man is not the spirit, nor the higher forms of consciousness, but the dark, unconscious drives in the human soul and that the historical fate of both individual and group depends primarily upon the continuity of these processes and their symbolic correlates—just as the dark world of the myth is not a product of history but rather an influential, determining factor in the course of history. All these theories, however, are mistaken in deriving from the world of drives, not only the energy and activity of the spirit, and its ideas and values, but also the ideas themselves in their essential meaning, and even the laws of the spirit and its inner growth. If traditional idealism of the classical theory overestimated the power of spirit and overlooked Spinoza's truth that reason is incapable of ruling the passions except in so far as it becomes a kind of "passion" through sublimation, as we would say today, then the naturalistic theories have erred in completely disregarding the originality and autonomy of the spirit.

In contrast to all these theories a recent writer, eccen-

* Schopenhauer, however, did not succumb to a full-fledged naturalism. His negative theory of man prevented this. [In the original this passage occurs in the text. Trans.]

tric but not without depth, has advanced a view not unlike our own according to which man is to be understood in terms of the two basic and irreducible categories of "life" and "spirit." * I refer to Ludwig Klages. It is he who is primarily responsible for providing the philosophical foundations for the pan-romantic conception of man which we now find among many thinkers in different scientific disciplines, for example, Edgar Dacqué, Leo Frobenius, C. G. Jung, H. Prinzhorn, Theodor Lessing and, to a certain extent, Oswald Spengler.

This view, which I will not analyze in detail, makes two major assertions: First, spirit is taken as an original phenomenon, but it is always identified, as in the case of the positivists and pragmatists, with intelligence and with the capacity to choose. Klages does not recognize that spirit originally not only objectifies but is also capable of obtaining a vision of ideas and essences by virtue of its capacity to cancel reality. Next, spirit thus deprived of its real essence is completely devalued. According to Klages, spirit and life are not complementary principles, but spirit is engaged, from the beginning and by its nature, in a struggle with life and with all psychic life of simple, automatic expressiveness. In this struggle, spirit appears as the principle which is more and more destructive of life and soul in the course of history. Thus history appears as decadence, as a record of a progressive disease of life as represented in man. If Klages were

* The distinction between spirit and life is already the basis of my first work, the "Transcendental and Psychological Method." It is also contained in my Ethics. The meaning of my terms differs from Klages' because he equates "spirit" with "intelligence," "ego" and "will."

consistent,* he would have put this "tragedy" of life which is man into the origin of man itself.

There cannot be such a dynamic and hostile polarity between life and spirit as is evident from the fact that spirit has no original power or active energy through which it could perform this work of "destruction." The evidence cited by Klages in his perceptive observations on some of the truly deplorable manifestations of late cultural periods in history does not reflect upon the spirit itself, but rather upon a process which I call "oversublimation." [8] This refers to a condition of an excessive intellectualization or cerebration, which produces the reaction of the romantic escape into a previous and often imaginary state in history when this oversublimation, and especially the excess of discursive, intellectual life, was not yet present. The Dionysian movement in Greece was such an escape, as was the movement of Hellenistic dogmatism which looked back to classical Greece as German romanticism looked back to the Middle Ages. Klages does not sufficiently appreciate the fact that these historical images are chiefly nourished by a longing for youth and primitivity (as a reaction to overintellectualization) and that they never coincide with historical reality. He also overlooks the fact that whenever we find a Dionysian state of human existence in its original and naive form,† this

* He is not [consistent] because, strangely enough, spirit "breaks into" history only at a certain point after the coming of man so that the history of Homo sapiens is preceded by an enormous prehistory viewed with the eyes of Bachofen. [In the original this passage occurs in the text. Trans.]

† We never find it in this form because, as we saw, a completely uninhibited state of the instinctive life is as much under the direction of the spirit as is an ascetic, rational repression. The animal does not

Dionysian state itself is based upon a complicated conscious technique of the will. In other words, it uses the very spirit that is to be put aside.

Another group of phenomena which Klages interprets as consequences of the destructive power of spirit indicates simply that whenever spiritual activities take the place of vital activities that run their course automatically, the latter, indeed, are disturbed considerably. Simple symptoms of this kind are, for example, the effect that attention may have on disturbing the heartbeat, on breathing or on other automatic or semiautomatic activities; again, the disturbances that occur when the will is directly opposed to vital impulses instead of aiming at new goals of value. But what Klages here calls "spirit" is not spirit in the strict sense, but only a complicated technical intelligence, as we have defined it previously. In this fundamental respect, Klages radically opposed as he is to all positivistic conceptions of man as *Homo faber*, adopts uncritically the view to which he is opposed. Spirit and life are complementary and interrelated. It is a fallacy to represent them as original enemies consumed in struggle with each other. "He who has thought most deeply loves that which is most alive." (Hölderlin).

---

know such a complete release of inhibitions. [In the original this passage occurs in the text. Trans.]

IV philosophical anthropology and religion

It would be the task of a philosophical anthropology to show in detail how all the specific achievements and works of man—language, conscience, tools, weapons, ideas of right and wrong, the state, leadership, the representational function of art, myths, religion, science, history and social life—arise from the basic structure of the human nature as we have briefly described it in this essay. This cannot be done here. We can, however, take a look at some of the consequences that follow from what we have said with regard to the relationship between man and the Ground of Being.

One of the finest results of this analysis of the successive stages in the structure of human nature as it emerges from lower stages of existence is to indicate the inner necessity with which man, at the very moment he becomes human by virtue of his consciousness of the world and himself, and by virtue of his capacity to objectify his own psychophysical nature—the specific characteristics of the spirit—must also encounter the completely formal idea of an infinite absolute Being beyond this world. As soon as man has separated himself from the rest of nature and looks upon nature as an "object"—this belongs to his essence and constitutes the very act of becoming man—he must, then, turn around with a sense of awe and ask: "Where do I stand? What is my place in the universe?" Now he can no longer say: "I am part of the world and surrounded by it," for the actual reality of his spirit and his person passes beyond even the *forms* of being of this world in space and time. Thus, in this movement of turning around he looks, as it were, into nothingness. He discovers the possibility of an absolute nothingness, and this discovery drives him to ask: "Why is there a world as such, and why and how do I exist?" [1]

We should note the essential necessity of the relationship which holds between the consciousness of the world, self-consciousness, and the (formal) consciousness of God—where God is to be conceived as a being in itself (*causa sui*) to whom we attribute the predicate "holy," capable of manifesting itself in a thousand different ways. The sphere of an absolute Being as such, regardless of whether it is accessible to experience or knowledge, belongs to the essence of man just as much as self-consciousness and consciousness of the world. What von Humboldt said of language—that man could not have "invented" it because he is a human being only by virtue of having language—is just as applicable, with the same strictness, to the formal sphere of a Being, absolute in itself, that transcends all finite contents of experience and the central being of man himself, and that commands an awe-inspiring holiness. If the expression "the origin of religion" or "the origin of metaphysics" is not identified with any specific theoretical assumptions or doctrines of faith, but refers only to the origin of this sphere itself, then this origin would coincide with the origin of man himself.

Man discovers the peculiar accident or the contingency of the fact that there is a world rather than nothing, and that he exists instead of being nothing,[2] at the very moment he becomes conscious of the world and himself. Hence, it is a complete mistake to assert that I exist (as in Descartes) or that there is a world (as in St. Thomas Aquinas) before asserting the general proposition that there is an absolute Being—in other words, to derive the sphere of absolute Being from the other modes of being. Consciousness of the world, of the self and of God forms an inseparable structural unity, just as transcendence of the object and self-consciousness originate in the same act, the "third reflex" movement.

At the moment when the actual spiritual being and its ideal contents constituted themselves through the act of saying "No" to the concrete reality in the environment, when an attitude of world-openness originated and a never-ceasing urge to penetrate without limits into the revealed sphere of the world and to stop at nothing in the world of facts, when man, becoming himself, broke with the methods of all preceding life to adjust or to be adjusted to the environment and embarked upon the opposite direction of adapting the revealed world to himself and to his own life of organic stability, when man separated himself from nature and transformed it into an object subject to domination and to the control of symbolic manipulation—at this moment man was also driven to anchor his own central being in something beyond this world. He who had placed himself so boldly above this world could no longer regard himself merely as a "member" or "part" of this world.

After man had discovered both the contingency of the world and the curious accident that his own center of being transcended this world, it was still possible for him to take a twofold attitude: He could pause in wonder (θαυμάζειν) and then set his spirit in motion to grasp the Absolute and to become part of it. That is the origin of metaphysics of any kind. It has appeared late in history and only among a few peoples. Man could, however, take a different course: he could also yield to the irresistible urge for safety or protection, not only for himself, but primarily for the group as a whole. By means of the enormous surplus of fantasy which was his heritage in contrast to the animal, he could then populate this sphere of being with imaginary figures in order to seek refuge in their power through cult and ritual. The purpose was to get some protection and help "to back him up," since the basic act of his estrangement from, and his objectification of, nature—together with his self-consciousness—threatened to throw him into pure nothingness.

The overcoming of this nihilism by means of such protective measures is what we call religion. Religion is originally a group and collective phenomenon; only later, with the origin of the state, is it linked with a founder. Even as the world is originally given to us in a practical context, in the experience of resistance before it becomes an object of knowledge, so these ideas and images in the newly discovered sphere of being, from which mankind has drawn the strength to maintain itself in the world,* must historically precede

* Such help first came from mythology, later from religion detaching itself from myth. [In the original this passage occurs in the text. Trans.]

all forms of knowledge aiming at the truth as we find them in metaphysics.

Let us take a few of the major types of religious ideas that man has formed about the relationship between himself and the highest Ground of Being, and let us restrict ourselves to the stage of monotheism as developed in the Western World. We find conceptions such as making a "covenant" between man and God after God chose a special kind of people as his own (ancient Judaism). Or man appears, depending upon the structure of society, as a "slave of God," who prostrates himself with cunning and servile abasement and attempts to influence God through prayers, threats or magical practices. In a somewhat higher form he appears as "the faithful servant" of the supreme and sovereign Lord. The highest and purest conception possible within the limits of monotheism is the idea that all human beings are "children" of God, the "Father," through the mediation of the divine "Son" who has revealed to man the inner nature of God and who has prescribed to them, on divine authority, doctrines of faith and moral commands.

We reject all these conceptions on philosophical grounds. We must do so for the simple reason that we deny the basic presupposition of theism: a spiritual, personal God omnipotent in his spirituality. For us the basic relationship between man and the Ground of Being consists in the fact that this Ground comprehends and realizes itself directly in man, who, both as spirit and as life, is but a partial mode of the eternal spirit and drive.

This is an old idea which we find in Spinoza, Hegel and many other thinkers: the original Being becomes conscious of itself in man in the same act by which man sees himself grounded in this being. We need but transform this thought, previously presented too intellectualistically, so that man's knowledge of being so grounded is the result of the active commitment of our own being to the ideal demand of *deitas* and the attempt to fulfill this demand. In and through this fulfillment, man cooperates in the creation of God, who emerges from the Ground of Being in a process whereby spirit and drive interpenetrate increasingly.

The locus of this self-realization, or let us say, self-deification, as it were, for which the Being in itself strives and for the sake of which it pays the price of the world as "history"—this locus is man, the human self and the human heart. Here is the only place where the deification is accessible to us—but it is a genuine part of the transcendent process itself. For, although all things emerge in the process of continuous creation from the Ground of Being, from the functional unity of the cooperative interplay between spirit and drive, these two attributes of the Being in itself that are known to us are related to each other solely in man as a living unity. Man is the focus where they intersect.

The logos "according to" which the world comes into being becomes in man an act in which he can cooperate. Thus, according to this view, the birth of man and the birth of God are, from the outset, reciprocally dependent upon each other. Even as man cannot find his own determination without recognizing himself as a link in these two attributes of the highest Being and as dwelling within this Being itself, so this Being, too, cannot find its own determination without the cooperation of man. Spirit and drive, the two attributes of being, are not complete in themselves—quite aside from the incompleteness of their mutual interpenetration which is their goal. They also grow in themselves in the process of the history of the human spirit and in the evolution of life in the world.

I have heard it said that it is not possible for man to endure the idea of an unfinished God, or a God in the process of becoming. My answer is that metaphysics is not an insurance policy for those who are weak and in need of protection. It is something for strong and courageous minds. Thus it is understandable that man reaches the consciousness that he is an ally and co-worker of God only in the process of his own development and growing self-knowledge. The need for safety and protection by an omnipotent being, beyond man and the world, and identical with goodness and wisdom, is too great not to have broken through all barriers of sense and intelligence during the times of man's immaturity. This relationship is both childlike and weak. It has detached man from God and it is expressed in the objectifying and evasive relations of contemplation, worship and prayer. In place of this relationship we put the elementary act of a personal commitment to the deity, the self-identification of man with the active spiritual movement of the deity. The final actual "reality" of this Being in itself is not capable of objectification any more than the being of another person. One can take part in its life and spiritual actuality only through participation, through an act of commitment or active identification. Absolute Being does not have the function to protect or to complement man's weakness and needs which always want to make an "object" out of this being.

Yet, there is a kind of "support" even for us. This is

the support provided by the total process of realizing values in world history in so far as this process has moved forward toward the making of a "God." But we must not wait for theoretical certainties before we commit ourselves. It is the commitment of the person himself that opens up the possibility of "knowing" this Being in itself.

notes

If the reader wishes to learn something about the steps in the development of my views presented in this essay, I would recommend that he read: (1) the essays, "Zur Idee des Menschen" and "Das Ressentiment im Aufbau der Moralen," both included in the volume, *Vom Umsturz der Werte;* (2) the corresponding sections in my book, *Der Formalismus in der Ethik und die materielle Werthethik;* and on the subject of the specific qualities of human feelings, *The Nature of Sympathy;* (3) on the subject of man's relationship to history and society, my book, *Die Wissenformen und die Gesellschaft,* and the essay, "Man and History"; and (4) the essays, "Forms of Knowledge and Culture" and "Man in the Era of Adjustment." The last three essays are reprinted in *Philosophical Perspectives.**

INTRODUCTION: THE CONCEPT OF MAN

1. See the essay, "Zur Idee des Menschen" [*Vom Umsturz der Werte* (3rd ed.; Leipzig, 1923)]. Here it is shown that the traditional concept of man is based on the idea that he was created in the image of God. Hence, the idea is presupposed as a point of reference.

I THE STAGES OF PSYCHOPHYSICAL LIFE IN PLANT, ANIMAL AND MAN

1. See the essay, "Erkenntnis und Arbeit," in the volume, *Die Wissenformen und die Gesellschaft* [Leipzig, 1926], and the

* [*This passage appears in the preface of the original. I have transposed it to this section because most of the works referred to are cited again in the footnotes. Most of the major works cited are mentioned in my general introduction. Trans.*]

essay, "Idealismus-Realismus," in *Philosophischer Anzeiger* [(Bonn, 1927) II, 3].

2. See the essays, "Probleme einer Soziologie des Wissens," and "Erkenntnis und Arbeit," in *Die Wissenformen und die Gesellschaft [supra].*

3. For a criticism of hedonism and eudemonism, cf. *Der Formalismus in der Ethik und die materielle Werthethik* [1916 (4th ed.; Bern, 1954)].

4. On sexual impulse and sexual love, cf. *The Nature of Sympathy* [trans. Peter Heath (London, 1954)].

5. Cf. Wolfgang Köhler, *Abhandlungen der Preussischen Akademie der Wissenschaften.*

6. For the difference between "value" and (material) "good," cf. *op. cit. [supra* note 3].

II THE ESSENCE OF SPIRIT

1. Cf. Julius Stenzel, "Der Ursprung des Geistbegriffes bei den Griechen," in *Die Antike.*

2. Treated more thoroughly in the essay, "Idealismus-Realismus" [*op. cit., supra* I, note 1].

3. Cf. "Erkenntnis und Arbeit" and "Idealismus-Realismus" [*ibid.*].

4. Cf. Sigmund Freud, *Beyond the Pleasure Principle.*

III SPIRIT AND LIFE

1. Cf. Freud [*op. cit., supra*].

2. From a sociological point of view, the classical theory is a one-sided ideology, the ideology of an upper class: the bourgeoisie. Cf. "Probleme einer Soziologie des Wissens" [*op. cit., supra* I, note 2] and "Man in the Era of Adjustment" [*Philosophical Perspectives,* trans. Oscar A. Haac (Boston: Beacon Press, 1958)].

3. Cf. "Erkenntnis und Arbeit" [*supra* I, note 1].

4. Cf. "Probleme einer Soziologie des Wissens" [*supra* I, note 2.].

5. *Ibid.*

6. For a criticism of historical materialism, cf. *ibid.*

7. For a criticism of Freud's theory of love, cf. *op. cit. [supra* I, note 5].

8. For the problem of resublimation and oversublimation, cf. "Man in the Era of Adjustment" [*supra* note 2].

IV PHILOSOPHICAL ANTHROPOLOGY AND RELIGION

1. Cf. the chapter, "Vom Gegenstand der Philosophie und die philosophische Erkenntnishaltung," in the essay, "Vom Wesen der Philosophie," included in the volume, *Vom Ewigen im Menschen* [1921].

2. *Ibid.*

index

Adaptation, 11
Adler, Alfred, 59, 83
Aesthetics, 13
Alsberg, Paul, 57–59, 61
Alverdes, 19, 20
Animal, 11, 17, 31–35, 43–46, 49, 51, 78, 80; behavior, 38; as biological unit, 38; concept of, 7, 10; consciousness, 39, 42; ecstasy, 39; intelligence of, 35; and man, 58, 78; mechanism, 12; psyche of, 41, 71; and reality, 55; sense of space and time, 45–46; structure of, 13
Anthropology, xvi; philosophical, xx, xxiii–xxv, 3, 6, 88; theological, 5
Anxiety, 14, 54
Aquinas, St. Thomas, 64, 90
Aristotle, xxiii, xxvi, 11, 22, 63
Art, 83, 88
Asceticism, 54–56, 61
Association, laws of, 23–24, 82
Augustine, St., x, xiii, xix, 48
Averroes, 64

Beauty, 66
Becoming, 68, 71
Behavior, xxviii, 14–16, 22–23; habitual, 21–22; instinctive, 15–19, 21, 28–29; intelligent, 29, 31; organic, 77; preconscious, 27
Behaviorism, xv, 15
Being, xxii, xxxii, 94–95; Absolute, xxiii, xxxv, 50, 88–91, 94; finite, 71; forms of, 64, 66, 68, 70–71; Ground of, 36, 42, 47–48, 58, 66, 70, 88, 92–93; highest, 70, 93; in itself, 51, 56, 89, 93; modes of, 64; principles of, 62; and world, 70
Bergson, Henri, xiii, xxvii, xxix, xxxv
Binswanger, L., xviii
Biology, xiii, 4, 36, 60–61, 74–75
Bixler, Julius S., vii
Blaauw, 10
Bocheński, I. M., ix n, xvii n
Brentano, F., xvii
Buddha, xvi, xxxiii, 49, 52, 55, 57–58, 60
Bühler, Karl, 20
Buytendyk, 20

Cassirer, Ernest, x
Catholicism, xix, xxxv
Causality, xxxi, 79, 82–83
Chemistry, 73
Concepts, explanation of, 58–59
Conditioned reflex, 10, 19, 22–23, 33
Conscience, 69, 88
Consciousness, 9–12, 39, 48, 53, 58, 64, 72, 75–76, 78, 84, 88–89, 94
Cosmology, 64
Creation, 48, 70, 78, 93
Culture, 58, 60; human, 83; spiritual, xxi; Western, xxiii

Dacqué, Edgar, 85
Darwin, Charles, xx, 6, 12–13
Darwinian-Lamarckian school, 35
Democritus, 82
Descartes, René, xvi, 49, 71–72, 72 n, 73–76, 90
Dewey, John, xxvii, 82

Dilthey, Wilhem, xiii, xxvii
Dogmatism, 86
Dualism, xxxii, 70, 74–75, 80; of
life and spirit, xxxiv

Ecstasy, 11, 37, 39–41
Élan vital, xxvii
Empiricism, xiv, 82
Epicurus, 63, 82
Epistemology, xiii
Essence, xx, xxiii, xxix–xxx, 36,
48–51, 55, 57, 66, 85, 89; and ex-
istence, xvi, xxxi, 51
Ethics, xii–xiii, xvi–xvii, 58
Evil, 55
Evolution, xxvii, xxix, xxxv, 5, 26,
36, 68, 94; psychic, 20
Existentialism, xxiv
Experience, sensory, 18, 55, 82, 89

Fabre, J. H., 17
Faith, xxxv, 89
Fechner, Gustav, 9
Fichte, Johann Gottlieb, 63–64
Forms: hierarchy of, 42; inorganic,
41
Freedom, xxx, 37, 62
Freud, Sigmund, xviii, xxi, xxxiii–
xxxiv, 55, 57, 59–60, 63, 84
Frobenius, Leo, 85

Gestalt, xxviii, xxix
God, xviii, xix, xxiii, xxvi, xxxii,
xxxv, 57, 63, 89–90, 92–95
Godhead, 57
Goethe, Johann Wolfgang von, 47
Good, 55
"Guidance," 62

Haberlandt, Gottlieb, 10
Hartmann, Eduard von, 64
Hartmann, Nicolai, 65
Hedonism, 28
Hegel, G. W. F., xxii, xxiv, xxvi,
xxxv, 50–51, 63, 63 n, 64, 68, 83,
92
Heidegger, Martin, xiv, xv n
Hellenism, 86

Heyder, 76
Historicism, xiii
History, xxiv, 66, 68, 83, 86, 88, 93–
94; and reason, 68; world, 95;
conceptions of, xxi, xxxiii
Hobbes, Thomas, 63, 83
Hölderlin, Friedrich, 87
Holiness, 89
Holism, 74
Humanity, principle of, 58–59, 61
Humboldt, Wilhelm von, 89
Hume, David, xxix, 24, 33, 82
Husserl, Edmund, xiii–xiv, xv n,
xxxi, 52–54

Idealism: German, xiii, xxix; phil-
osophical, 48, 65, 84
Ideas, xxi–xxii
Ideation, xxxi, 49–51, 53, 71
Ideology, xiii
Immortality, 78
"Impulse," 9
Instinct, 14–18, 27–28, 31–33, 36,
38, 55, 59, 61, 69; death, 60
Intelligence, xxix, 16–17, 20–21,
27–31, 33, 35–36, 85, 87, 94; prac-
tical, 31, 49
Intuition, xxxi, of essences, 52; of
forms, 51–52; of space, 44; of
space and time, 44
Irrationalism, xxxiv

Jaensch, E. R., 33
James, William, 69, 82
Jaspers, Karl, xviii
Jennings, Herbert, 16, 19, 81
Judaism, 92
Judeo-Christian tradition, 5, 63
Jung, C. G., 85

Kant, Immanuel, xvii, xxviii, xxx–
xxxi, 47, 51, 64
Klages, Ludwig, xxxiv, 85–87
Knowledge, xxiii, 21, 50, 58, 91–
92; a priori, 51; historical, 26;
sacred, 60; scientific, xxiii; sociology of, xxii
Köhler, Wolfgang, xvii, 30–31

Lamarck, 13, 61
Lamettrie, Julien Offroy de, 63, 82
Laws, 74–75, 83; of association, 23–24, 82; natural, 67; physical, 82; of thought, 82
Leibnitz, Gottfried Wilhelm von, 40, 51
Lessing, Theodor, 85
Libido, xxxi, xxxiii, 60, 83
Life, xxiv, xxxiv, 72; forms of, 75; instinctive, 82; plant, 23; process of, 78; psychic, 8–9, 19, 22–23, 25, 31, 36, 53, 71–74, 78; and spirit, xxxv, 56–87; unity of, 78
Linnaeus, 6
Locke, John, 24
Loeb, Jacques, 19
Logic, xiii, 50
Logos, 5 n, 93
Lotze, Rudolph, 75
Love, xviii, 51; eternal, 48; Platonic-Augustinian view of, xviii; sexual, 84
Lucretius, 82

Mach, Ernst, 58, 82
Machiavelli, 63, 83
Magic, 92
Man: affinity with the plant, 14; and animal, 29, 58–61, 65, 91; behavior, 39; characteristics, 43; concept of, 5–6, 87; culture-producing activities of, 57; definition of, 58; Dionysian state, 86; drives in, 18; and environment, 59; essence of, 89; the eternal Faust, 55; evolution of, 68; expression in, 12; and God, 92–94; idea of, xxiii, 56; and instinct, 55; intelligence of, 36; and nature, xx, 88; nature of, 36, 51, 64, 71, 88; organization, 45; origin of, 90; as person, 46; primitive, 41; psychic structure of, xxx; romantic conception of, 85; self-consciousness, 40; spirit of, xxi–xxii, 42, 54–56, 64; as spirit-

ual being, 46; structure of, 3–4; theories of, xii, 81; vitalistic conception of, 83; and world, xxx, 90–91
Mannheim, Karl, xxii
Marx, Karl, xxi–xxii, 63, 68, 83
Materialism, 64
Mathematics, xiii, xvi, 49, 72
Matter 71; and form, 64; prime, 63
Mechanism, 65, 67, 70, 72, 74, 76, 81–82, 84
Memory, 18, 22, 52; associative, 22–25, 30, 36
Mendel, 78–79
Merleau-Ponty, xviii
Metaphysics, x, xviii, xxiii, 6, 13, 35, 50, 58, 80, 89, 91–92, 94
Meyerhoff, Hans, viii
Middle Ages, 86
Mill, John Stuart, 24
Mind, 62, 71; body problem, 73, 80
Monism, xxxii
Monotheism, 92
Moore, G. E., xvii
Morphogenesis, 17–18
Mysticism, 62
Myth, 84, 88

Naturalism, xiii–xiv, xviii, xx–xxi, xxvii, xxxii, xxxiv, 63–64, 81, 84, 84 n
Nature, xxii, xxix–xxx, xxxv, 67, 69, 72, 74, 90–91; and spirit, xxiv; contingencies of, 65; human, 71
Nazis, ix
Nietzsche, Friedrich, xiii, xxi–xxii, xxix, xxxiv, 11, 41, 82–83
Nirvana, 57

Objectification, 47
Objects, xxviii, 37, 39, 63, 67, 89–90
Ontology, 35, 67, 74, 78
Organism, 42, 73, 76, 81–82
Oversoul, 25

Pacifism, xi
Pantheism, xxxv, 63
Pascal, x, xiii
Paul, St., 69
Pavlov, Ivan, 23
Peirce, Charles S., xi, 82
Person, xxxi, xxxiii, 36–37, 42, 47, 56, 95
Phenomenology, xiii–xv, xix–xx, xxv, xxix, xxxi, xxxiv, 77; analysis, xvii–xviii, xx; method of reduction, xv, xxxi, 52
Philistinism, 55
Philosophy, xv, xix, xxxi, 3, 54, 83; German, ix; of history, 83; of life, xiii, xx; of religion, ix; Oxford Linguistic, xiv n; Western, 62
Physics, 67, 74
Physiology, 49, 73–77, 79
Plants, 16, 42, 60, 65, 71; affinity with man, 14; behavior, 12–13; concept of, 9–11; ecstasy, 11, 39; expression, 12; mechanism, 12; memory, 10
Plato, x, xxiv, 52, 54, 63
Pleasure principle, 57
Positivism, 85, 87
Pragmatism, 82, 85
Prinzhorn, H., 85
Psychology, xiii, xvi, 4–5, 14–15, 24, 36, 74
Psychotherapy, 77

Rathenau, Walter, x
Rationalism, 54
Realism, xix
Reality, xxxii, 14, 51–56, 66, 85; experience of, 52–54; sense of, 53
Reason, 51, 67, 84; in history, xxxv, 5; human, 27; and spirit, 36, 58, 61–62
Reflex arc, xxviii, 21
Reinarus, 21
Religion, xiii, xvi, xix, xxiv, xxvi, 88–89, 91

Repression, xxxi, xxxiii, 55–57, 59, 61–62; sublimated, 61, 79
Romanticism, xxxiv; German, 86
Russell, Bertrand, xi

Salvation, xxiii, xxxiv, 57
Sartre, Jean-Paul, xviii, xxvi
Scheler, Maria, vii
Scheler, Max: Biography, ix–xi; convert to Catholicism, xix n; doctrine of man, xxv–xxvi; idea of man, xii, xxiii, xxix; influence of phenomenology, xiv–xvi; as man of passion, x–xi, xx; personality, ix–x; philosophical achievements, xxv; thought of, ix–xxxv
Schelling, 64
Schilder, 27 n
Schiller, 54, 82
Scholasticism, 75
Schopenhauer, Arthur, xxxiii, 57–60, 63, 84
Schutz, Alfred, xi n
Science, xiii, xv–xvi, xxiv–xxv, xxxi, 5–6, 45–46, 75, 83, 88; empirical, x; experimental, xxiii; historical, 27; natural, 7, 73, 78; physical, 82; social, x
Self, and ego, 73
Self-consciousness, xxx, 4–5, 40, 42, 89–91
Sex, 28, 77, 83–84
Sklarek, Ursula, viii
Sociology, xiii, xvi, xx, xxv, 4; of knowledge, xxii
Soul, xxxii, 47, 52, 64, 72, 74–75, 78, 80–81, 84; as world-soul, xxxii
Space, xxxi, 44–45, 51, 53, 58, 89; manifold, 45; world, 46
Spencer, Herbert, 19
Spengler, Oswald, 85
Spinoza, xxvii, xxxv, 64, 69, 84, 92
Spirit, xxi–xxii, xxx–xxxii, xxxiv, 36, 37, 39, 47–51, 54–55, 88–89;

as all-powerful, 63; autonomy of, 62–63, 72; form of, 56; and instinct, 55; and intellect, 48; and life, xxxv, 56–87; of man, 68; and object, 47; and psyche, 47; and reason, 36, 72 n; theory of, xxxii–xxxiii; as unique, 60
Sublimation, xxxi, xxxii, 55–56, 61–62, 66–69, 71, 79, 84
Substance, xxx, 43, 71, 73–74, 82
Symbols, 26, 44, 59, 61, 84, 90

Technology, xxiv, 78
Teleology, 13, 48, 65, 70
Theism, xix, xxxv, 13, 63, 71, 78, 92
Theology, 5, 65
Thomism, xix
Thought, 51
Time, xxxi, 51, 58, 66, 89
Tradition, 26–27

Universe, 46, 57, 89

Vaihinger, Hans, 83
Values, xii, xvi–xviii, xxxii, 21, 30, 34, 48, 51, 60–61, 65–66, 68, 71, 84, 95; objective, xxxi, 48
Veblen, Thorstein, xi
Vitalism, xiii, 65, 81–82, 84
Vogt, Karl, 83

"Whole," xxvii
"World," xxx–xxxi, 37, 39–40, 52–55, 67, 70–71, 88–90, 93–94; as given, 52; inorganic, 64–66, 68; laws of, 46; organic, 72; realization, 48; sensory, 52, 58; space, 44; structures of, 50; view, 45, 57, 64–65, 70; Western, 63, 65, 78, 92
World-ground, 70
World War I, x
Wundt, Wilhelm, 19